CW01523468

THE EVERYDAY KETO DIET COOKBOOK

Tasty and Healthy Recipes Using Metric Measurements to Begin Your Keto Adventure with a Complete 4-Week Meal Plan | Full Colour Edition

Judy K. Silas

Copyright© 2024 By Judy K. Silas Rights Reserved

This book is copyright protected. It is only for personal use. You cannot amend, distribute, sell, use, quote or paraphrase any part of the content within this book, without the consent of the author or publisher.

Under no circumstances will any blame or legal responsibility be held against the publisher, or author, for any damages, reparation, or monetary loss due to the information contained within this book, either directly or indirectly.

Limit of Liability/Disclaimer of Warranty:

No book, including this one, can ever replace the diagnostic expertise and medical advice of a physician in providing information about your health. The information contained herein is not intended to replace medical advice. You should consult with your doctor before using the information in this or any health-related book.

The Publisher and the author make no representations or warranties with respect to the accuracy or completeness of the contents of this work and specifically disclaim all warranties, including without limitation warranties of fitness for a particular purpose. No warranty may be created or extended by sales or promotional materials. The advice and strategies contained herein may not be suitable for every situation. This work is sold with the understanding that the Publisher is not engaged in rendering medical, legal, or other professional advice or services. If professional assistance is required, the services of a competent professional person should be sought. Neither the Publisher nor the author shall be liable for damages arising here from. The fact that an individual, organization, or website is referred to in this work as a citation and/or potential source of further information does not mean that the author or the Publisher endorses the information the individual, organization, or website may provide or recommendations they/ it may make. Further, readers should be aware that websites listed in this work may have changed or disappeared between when this work was written and when it is read.

Manufactured in the United Kingdom
Interior and Cover Designer: Danielle Rees
Art Producer: Brooke White
Editor: Aaliyah Lyons
Production Editor: Sienna Adams
Production Manager: Sarah Johnson
Photography: Michael Smith

TABLE OF CONTENTS

TABLE OF CONTENTS

TABLE OF CONTENTS

INTRODUCTION

When I first heard about the Keto diet, I have to admit, I wasn't particularly interested. A fitness trainer had recommended it to me, but the idea of making such a big change to my diet didn't seem appealing. I was sceptical—how could something so different possibly work? But, after a few more chats with the trainer and seeing some of the success stories, I decided to give it a go. At worst, I thought, it'd be a short-term experiment.

The first couple of weeks were tough. I really missed the familiar routine of my old eating habits. But after a while, things started to change. I felt more energised, my body wasn't sluggish after meals, and the weight seemed to be shifting slowly but surely. The real surprise came when I had my body metrics checked, and the results were astonishing—better muscle tone, reduced fat percentage, and more energy than I had in years.

Fast forward to today, and Keto has become a way of life for me. Not only have I stuck with it, but I also recommend it to my family and friends. I've even started sharing my favourite Keto recipes with them—ones that have been tried and tested over time. It's been rewarding to see the positive impact it's had on others as well, and I love being able to offer guidance from my own experience. The transformation has been so much more than just physical—Keto has become part of my lifestyle.

DEDICATION

I want to thank you, Amanda, my fitness trainer, for your unwavering support and guidance throughout my Keto journey. Your expertise has been invaluable, and your encouragement has kept me on track, helping me take fewer detours along the way. I truly appreciate your patience in answering my questions and offering personalised advice whenever I needed it. You've given me the confidence to persevere, even during the tougher moments, and I'm so grateful for that. Thanks to you, I've not only embraced Keto but also seen incredible results, and I'll always be thankful for your role in this transformation.

CHAPTER 1: GETTING STARTED WITH KETO DIET

DEMYSTIFYING THE LOW-CARB, HIGH-FAT LIFESTYLE

The Keto diet can sound quite different from what we're used to hearing about food and weight loss. It's all about shifting the way your body fuels itself by drastically reducing carbohydrates and increasing fat intake. The idea is simple, but its effects on the body are profound. Let's take a closer look at the science behind it and how it changes your metabolism.

THE SCIENCE OF KETOSIS: HOW YOUR BODY SWITCHES FUEL SOURCES

Normally, your body uses carbohydrates as its primary source of energy. When you eat foods like bread, pasta, or rice, your body breaks them down into glucose (sugar), which it uses for energy. However, when you cut back on carbs—like in the Keto diet—your body runs out of glucose to burn. This is where the magic happens.

In the absence of glucose, your body begins to look for an alternative fuel source: fat. This process is called ketosis. During ketosis, your liver breaks down fat into molecules called ketones, which your brain and body can use for energy instead of glucose. Essentially, you're training your body to run on fat rather than carbs.

Ketosis is a completely natural state, and while it might take a few days for your body to adapt, once you're there, many people feel more energised and focused. This shift in energy sources also leads to fat burning, making Keto an effective way to lose weight for many people.

KEY PRINCIPLES OF THE KETO DIET AND HOW IT RESHAPES METABOLISM

The Keto diet focuses on high-fat, moderate-protein, and very low-carb foods. The goal is to make fat your main fuel source instead of carbohydrates. Here's how the principles work:

LOW-CARB, HIGH-FAT DIET

In a standard Keto plan, you aim to get about 70-80% of your daily calories from fats, 15-25% from protein, and just 5-10% from carbs. This dramatic reduction in carbohydrates forces your body to adapt, eventually entering ketosis. Foods you'll eat regularly include fatty cuts of meat, full-fat dairy, avocados, nuts, and oils, while you limit starchy foods like potatoes, bread, and pasta.

MODERATE PROTEIN INTAKE

Unlike some diets that recommend very high protein, the Keto diet suggests a moderate intake of protein. Too much protein can interfere with ketosis because the body can convert excess protein into glucose, preventing the switch to fat burning. Keto focuses on just the right amount of protein to support muscle maintenance without compromising fat burning.

RESHAPING YOUR METABOLISM

By reducing carbs and increasing fat intake, Keto changes the way your body processes food. It shifts your metabolism from being sugar-dependent to fat-dependent. This can lead to a more efficient fat-burning process, even when you're not working out. Additionally, the increased ketone production helps regulate hunger, making it easier to stick to a reduced-calorie intake without feeling deprived.

Your metabolism becomes more flexible as it adapts to burning fat for fuel. This means your body can better utilise stored fat, especially around stubborn areas like your abdomen, which often leads to weight loss. Many people also report feeling more mentally clear and less fatigued during the day, as the steady flow of ketones to the brain provides a consistent energy source.

THE BENEFITS YOU CAN'T IGNORE

The Keto diet offers more than just weight loss; it brings a range of life-changing health benefits that can improve your energy, mental clarity, and overall well-being. Here, we'll explore why the Keto diet works where other diets often fail, and we'll bust some common myths about what it can truly do for you.

LIFE-CHANGING HEALTH BENEFITS: MORE ENERGY, BETTER FOCUS, AND WEIGHT LOSS

One of the most noticeable benefits of the Keto diet is **increased energy**. Once your body adapts to burning fat for fuel instead of carbs, you'll find that your energy levels become much more stable throughout the day. This is because fat provides a steady, long-lasting source of energy, while carbs can cause spikes and crashes in blood sugar levels. Many people on Keto report feeling more alert and less fatigued, even without the need for caffeine or sugar.

Mental clarity is another benefit that many people experience. The brain thrives on ketones, which are produced when your body is in ketosis. Ketones are a more efficient fuel source for the brain than glucose, which can lead to clearer thinking, better focus, and improved concentration. This is particularly beneficial for people who struggle with brain fog or difficulty focusing throughout the day.

And, of course, **weight loss** is one of the primary reasons many people turn to Keto. The shift to fat burning means that your body starts to use stored fat as its main energy source. Many people experience significant weight loss, especially in the initial stages, as their bodies shed excess water weight and start breaking down fat. Keto can also help reduce visceral fat (the fat stored around organs), which is linked to various health issues such as heart disease and diabetes.

WHY KETO WORKS WHERE OTHER DIETS FAIL

So, why does Keto work when other diets often don't? The answer lies in the way Keto changes your metabolism. Most traditional diets focus on cutting calories or reducing fat intake, which can lead to slower metabolism over time. When you eat carbs, your body uses glucose for energy, but it quickly burns through this energy, leading to hunger and cravings.

Keto, on the other hand, changes your body's fuel source from glucose to fat. This allows you to feel fuller for longer periods, reducing the temptation to snack or overeat. Because Keto is a high-fat, low-carb diet, it stabilises your blood sugar and insulin levels, which helps curb cravings and appetite.

Additionally, Keto is sustainable in the long run because it encourages a balanced intake of fats, protein, and very few carbs. You're not left feeling hungry or deprived, which is often the case with low-calorie diets or restrictive eating plans. The result is that many people find it easier to stick to

the Keto lifestyle, allowing for lasting weight loss and health improvements.

BUSTING THE MYTHS: WHAT KETO CAN REALLY DO FOR YOU

There are plenty of myths surrounding the Keto diet, so it's important to separate fact from fiction. One common myth is that **eating so much fat can lead to heart disease**. While it's true that consuming unhealthy fats (like trans fats or excessive processed oils) can be harmful, the Keto diet encourages healthy fats such as those found in avocados, olive oil, and fatty fish. These fats are beneficial for heart health and help reduce inflammation in the body.

Another myth is that **Keto is just a fad diet**. In reality, the Keto diet has been used for nearly a century to treat epilepsy, and more recent research shows that it can have numerous other health benefits, such as improved insulin sensitivity and support for those with Type 2 diabetes. Keto is also being studied for its potential to help manage neurological conditions like Alzheimer's and Parkinson's disease.

Some people also fear that **Keto is too restrictive**. While it's true that Keto requires cutting out high-carb foods, it doesn't mean you're limited to eating bland or boring meals. In fact, Keto offers a wide variety of delicious foods, including meats, fish, cheese, eggs, nuts, and plenty of low-carb vegetables. Once you learn the ropes, you'll find that there's a wealth of tasty options to choose from.

SIMPLE STEPS TO START YOUR KETO JOURNEY

Starting the Keto diet doesn't have to be complicated. With a few simple steps, you can begin your journey to better health and weight loss. In this section, we'll break down the essentials of macronutrients—carbs, fat, and protein—and provide tips to make the transition into Keto as smooth as possible.

UNDERSTANDING MACRONUTRIENTS: CARB, FAT, AND PROTEIN BALANCE

The Keto diet revolves around adjusting your intake of three main macronutrients: **carbohydrates, fats,** and **protein**. The key to success on Keto is getting the right balance between these, with a heavy emphasis on fats and a sharp reduction in carbs.

CARBOHYDRATES

On a typical Keto diet, carbohydrates make up only about 5-10% of your daily calorie intake. This is much lower than what you might be used to. The goal is to reduce your carb consumption to a level where your body starts using fat as its primary fuel source, rather than glucose from carbs. Common high-carb foods like bread, pasta, rice, and sugary treats should be avoided. Instead, you'll focus on **low-carb vegetables** (like spinach, kale, and cauliflower) and **small portions of berries** when you need a sweet treat.

FATS

Fats are the cornerstone of the Keto diet, making up 70-80% of your daily calorie intake. But it's important to focus on healthy fats—these include fats from avocados, olive oil, coconut oil, butter, and fatty cuts of meat. These fats not only provide your body with the energy it needs but also help keep you feeling full and satisfied. They're also essential for keeping your hormones balanced and supporting brain function.

PROTEIN

Protein should make up about 15-25% of your daily intake. Unlike some other low-carb diets that might encourage higher protein, Keto focuses on **moderate protein intake**. Too much protein can interfere with ketosis, as the body can convert excess protein into glucose. It's important to eat high-quality sources of protein such as eggs, lean meats, fish, and plant-based proteins like tofu or tempeh. Protein helps maintain muscle mass while you're losing fat, which is crucial for staying healthy during weight loss.

Balancing these macronutrients properly is the key to entering and staying in ketosis. By cutting carbs significantly and eating enough fats and protein, your body will begin to rely on fat for energy instead of carbs.

TRANSITIONING INTO KETO: TIPS FOR A SMOOTH START

Starting Keto can feel like a big shift, but with the right approach, the transition can be much easier. Here are some practical tips to help you get started and make the process as smooth as possible:

GRADUALLY REDUCE CARBS

While some people dive straight into Keto, others prefer to reduce their carb intake gradually. This can help avoid the dreaded "Keto flu," a temporary set of symptoms (like headaches, fatigue, or irritability) that some people experience when they suddenly cut carbs. Start by eliminating obvious sources of carbs, like sugary drinks and snacks, and slowly reduce your intake of grains and starchy vegetables. This way, your body has time to adjust to the new fuel source.

STAY HYDRATED AND GET ENOUGH SALT

When you reduce carbs, your body tends to lose more water and salt, which can lead to dehydration and an electrolyte imbalance. Make sure to drink plenty of water throughout the day. You may also want to add extra salt to your food or drink an electrolyte supplement to maintain proper fluid balance. This is especially important in the first few weeks as your body adapts.

PLAN YOUR MEALS

One of the biggest challenges of starting Keto is knowing what to eat. Meal planning can be a huge help. Focus on meals that are high in healthy fats, moderate in protein, and low in carbs. For example, you might have a breakfast of scrambled eggs with avocado and spinach, a salad with grilled chicken and olive oil dressing for lunch, and a dinner of salmon with a side of roasted vegetables. Having a variety of recipes on hand will make sticking to Keto easier.

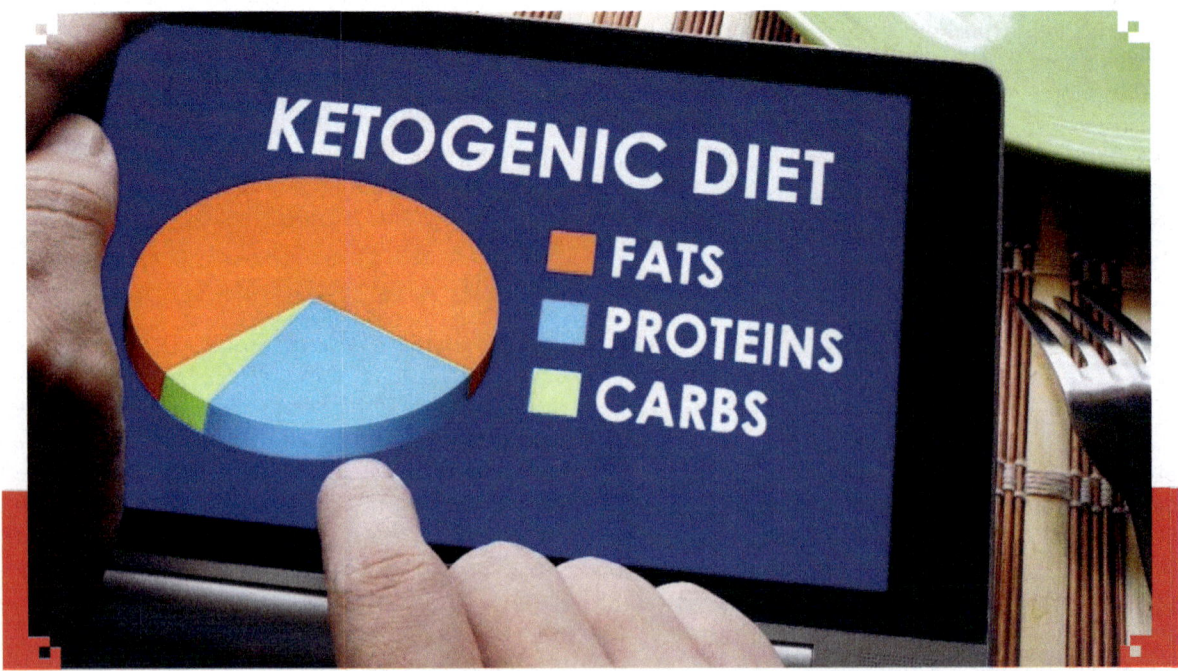

FOODS TO AVOID AND ENJOY ON THE KETO DIET

KETO FOODS TO ENJOY
HIGH FAT / LOW CARB (BASED ON NET CARBS)

MEATS & SEAFOOD
- Beef (ground beef, steak, etc.)
- Chicken
- Crab
- Crawfish
- Duck
- Fish
- Goose
- Lamb
- Lobster
- Mussels
- Octopus
- Pork (pork chops, bacon, etc.)
- Quail
- Sausage (without fillers)
- Scallops
- Shrimp
- Veal
- Venison

DAIRY
- Blue cheese dressing
- Burrata cheese
- Cottage cheese
- Cream cheese
- Eggs
- Greek yogurt (full-fat)
- Grilling cheese
- Halloumi cheese
- Heavy (whipping) cream
- Homemade whipped cream
- Kefalotyri cheese
- Mozzarella cheese
- Provolone cheese
- Queso blanco
- Ranch dressing
- Ricotta cheese
- Unsweetened almond milk
- Unsweetened coconut milk

VEGETABLES
- Alfalfa sprouts
- Asparagus
- Avocados
- Bell peppers
- Broccoli
- Cabbage
- Carrots (in moderation)
- Cauliflower
- Celery
- Chicory
- Coconut
- Cucumbers
- Garlic (in moderation)
- Green beans
- Herbs
- Jicama
- Lemons
- Limes
- Mushrooms
- Okra
- Olives
- Onions (in moderation)
- Pickles
- Pumpkin
- Radishes
- Salad greens
- Scallions
- Spaghetti squash (in moderation)
- Tomatoes (in moderation)
- Zucchini

NUTS & SEEDS
- Almonds
- Brazil nuts
- Chia seeds
- Flaxseeds
- Hazelnuts
- Macadamia nuts
- Peanuts (in moderation)
- Pecans
- Pine nuts
- Pumpkin seeds
- Sacha inchi seeds
- Sesame seeds
- Walnuts

FRUITS
- Blackberries
- Blueberries
- Cranberries
- Raspberries
- Strawberries

KETO FOODS TO AVOID
LOW FAT / HIGH CARB (BASED ON NET CARBS)

MEATS & MEAT ALTERNATIVES
- Deli meat (some, not all)
- Hot dogs (with fillers)
- Sausage (with fillers)
- Seitan
- Tofu

DAIRY
- Almond milk (sweetened)
- Coconut milk (sweetened)
- Milk
- Soy milk (regular)
- Yogurt (regular)

NUTS & SEEDS
- Cashews
- Chestnuts
- Pistachios

VEGETABLES
- Artichokes
- Beans (all varieties)
- Burdock root
- Butternut squash
- Chickpeas
- Corn
- Edamame
- Eggplant
- Leeks
- Parsnips
- Plantains
- Potatoes
- Sweet potatoes
- Taro root
- Turnips
- Winter squash
- Yams

FRUITS &
- Apples
- Apricots
- Bananas
- Boysenberries
- Cantaloupe
- Cherries
- Currants
- Dates
- Elderberries
- Gooseberries
- Grapes
- Honeydew melon
- Huckleberries
- Kiwifruits
- Mangos
- Oranges
- Peaches
- Peas
- Pineapples
- Plums
- Prunes
- Raisins
- Water chestnuts

KETO COOKING STAPLES
1. Pink Himalayan salt
2. Freshly ground black pepper
3. Ghee (clarified butter, without dairy; buy grass-fed if you can)
4. Olive oil
5. Grass-fed butter

KETO PERISHABLES
1. Eggs (pasture-raised, if you can)
2. Avocados
3. Bacon (uncured)
4. Cream cheese (full-fat; or use a dairy-free alternative)
5. Sour cream (full-fat; or use a dairy-free alternative)
6. Heavy whipping cream or coconut milk (full-fat; I buy the coconut milk in a can)
7. Garlic (fresh or pre-minced in a jar)
8. Cauliflower
9. Meat (grass-fed, if you can)
10. Greens (spinach, kale, or arugula)

7

CHAPTER 2: 4-WEEK MEAL PLAN

WEEK 1

Day 1:

Breakfast: Strawberry Chantilly Crêpes

Lunch: Creamy Cod with Jammy Onions & Dill

Snack: Salsa Cheese Party Dip

Dinner: Salsa Verde Chicken Tray Bake

Total for the day:

Calories: 1749; **Carbs:** 28.0 g; **Fibre:** 7.6 g; **Protein:** 75.9 g; **Fat:** 150.3 g

Day 2:

Breakfast: Cream-Baked Eggs

Lunch: Superfood Keto Salad

Snack: Cheddar & Chive Cauliflower Bites (2 serves)

Dinner: Creamy Cod with Jammy Onions & Dill

Total for the day:

Calories: 1727; **Carbs:** 30.9 g; **Fibre:** 15.6 g; **Protein:** 84.4 g; **Fat:** 141.0 g

Day 3:

Breakfast: Strawberry Chantilly Crêpes

Lunch: Salsa Verde Chicken Tray Bake

Snack: Salsa Cheese Party Dip (2 serves)

Dinner: Superfood Keto Salad

Total for the day:

Calories: 1940; **Carbs:** 38.2 g; **Fibre:** 13.5 g; **Protein:** 73.9 g; **Fat:** 163.3 g

Day 4:

Breakfast: Strawberry Coconut Smoothie

Lunch: Creamy Cod with Jammy Onions & Dill

Snack: Cheddar & Chive Cauliflower Bites

Dinner: Garlic-Parmesan Chicken

Total for the day:

Calories: 1849; **Carbs:** 27.0 g; **Fibre:** 6.3 g; **Protein:** 75.7 g; **Fat:** 162.5 g

Day 5:

Breakfast: Strawberry Coconut Smoothie

Lunch: Superfood Keto Salad

Snack: Salsa Cheese Party Dip

Dinner: Salsa Verde Chicken Tray Bake

Total for the day:

Calories: 1709; **Carbs:** 34.2 g; **Fibre:** 11.6 g; **Protein:** 58.9 g; **Fat:** 154.3 g

Day 6:

Breakfast: Cream-Baked Eggs

Lunch: Garlic-Parmesan Chicken

Snack: Cheddar & Chive Cauliflower Bites

Dinner: Creamy Cod with Jammy Onions & Dill

Total for the day:

Calories: 1784; **Carbs:** 17.7 g; **Fibre:** 6.3 g; **Protein:** 87.7 g; **Fat:** 151.5 g

Day 7:

Breakfast: Strawberry Chantilly Crêpes

Lunch: Salsa Verde Chicken Tray Bake

Snack: Roast Beef & Olive Spinach Rolls (2 serves)

Dinner: Superfood Keto Salad

Total for the day:

Calories: 1996; **Carbs:** 48.2 g; **Fibre:** 29.6 g; **Protein:** 93.9 g; **Fat:** 163.3 g

WEEK 2

Day 1:

Breakfast: Italian-Style Abundance Bowls

Lunch: Spicy Lamb Traybake with Celeriac Roasties

Snack: Peanut Butter and Jelly Ice Cream

Dinner: Avocado & Halloumi Salad

Total for the day:

Calories: 2002; **Carbs:** 45.1 g; **Fibre:** 14.5 g; **Protein:** 81.8 g; **Fat:** 169.2 g

Day 2:

Breakfast: Nut Butter Cream Shake

Lunch: 'Dirty Rice' with Bacon & Mushrooms

Snack: Tuna Avocado Boats with Lime (2 **serves**)

Dinner: Avocado & Bacon Salad

Total for the day:

Calories: 1898; **Carbs:** 31.6 g; **Fibre:** 20.1 g; **Protein:** 108.2 g; **Fat:** 152.7 g

Day 3:

Breakfast: Coconut and Almond Granola

Lunch: Avocado & Bacon Salad

Snack: Peanut Butter and Jelly Ice Cream

Dinner: Spicy Lamb Traybake with Celeriac Roasties

Total for the day:

Calories: 1755; **Carbs:** 45.4 g; **Fibre:** 15.1 g; **Protein:** 62.8 g; **Fat:** 161.7 g

Day 4:

Breakfast: Italian-Style Abundance Bowls

Lunch: Avocado & Bacon Salad

Snack: Tuna Avocado Boats with Lime

Dinner: 'Dirty Rice' with Bacon & Mushrooms

Total for the day:

Calories: 1718; **Carbs:** 30.1 g; **Fibre:** 16.6 g; **Protein:** 111.4 g; **Fat:** 131.9 g

Day 5:

Breakfast: Coconut and Almond Granola

Lunch: 'Dirty Rice' with Bacon & Mushrooms

Snack: Peanut Butter and Jelly Ice Cream

Dinner: Avocado & Halloumi Salad

Total for the day:

Calories: 1978; **Carbs:** 77.4 g; **Fibre:** 23 g; **Protein:** 63 g; **Fat:** 166 g

Day 6:

Breakfast: Nut Butter Cream Shake

Lunch: Spicy Lamb Traybake with Celeriac Roasties

Snack: Tuna Avocado Boats with Lime

Dinner: Avocado & Bacon Salad

Total for the day:

Calories: 1765; **Carbs:** 20.6 g; **Fibre:** 11.1 g; **Protein:** 78.2 g; **Fat:** 151.7 g

Day 7:

Breakfast: Coconut and Almond Granola

Lunch: 'Dirty Rice' with Bacon & Mushrooms

Snack: Peanut Butter and Jelly Ice Cream

Dinner: Spicy Lamb Traybake with Celeriac Roasties

Total for the day:

Calories: 1780; **Carbs:** 49.3 g; **Fibre:** 13 g; **Protein:** 69 g; **Fat:** 147 g

WEEK 3

Day 1:

Breakfast: Cheesy Spinach and Mushroom Scramble

Lunch: Ultimate Beef Stroganoff

Snack: Bacon-Wrapped Avocado Bites

Dinner: Egg Roll in a Bowl

Total for the day:

Calories: 1978; **Carbs:** 30.9 g; **Fibre:** 11.0 g; **Protein:** 97.0 g; **Fat:** 165.3 g

Day 2:

Breakfast: Overnight Chia Pots

Lunch: Egg Roll in a Bowl

Snack: Bacon-Wrapped Avocado Bites

Dinner: Ultimate Beef Stroganoff

Total for the day:

Calories: 1801; **Carbs:** 38.0 g; **Fibre:** 17.9 g; **Protein:** 78.6 g; **Fat:** 149.0 g

Day 3:

Breakfast: Avocado & Almond Butter Power Smoothie

Lunch: Egg Roll in a Bowl

Snack: Spicy Almond & Cheese Fat Bombs

Dinner: Cucumber & Smoked Salmon Salad

Total for the day:

Calories: 1774; **Carbs:** 30.2 g; **Fibre:** 14.1 g; **Protein:** 69.1 g; **Fat:** 140.4 g

Day 4:

Breakfast: Avocado & Almond Butter Power Smoothie

Lunch: Apple-Glazed Pork Rack

Snack: Spicy Almond & Cheese Fat Bombs

Dinner: Egg Roll in a Bowl

Total for the day:

Calories: 1924; **Carbs:** 31.1 g; **Fibre:** 14.7 g; **Protein:** 74.7 g **Fat:** 163.7 g

Day 5:

Breakfast: Cheesy Spinach and Mushroom Scramble

Lunch: Apple-Glazed Pork Rack

Snack: Bacon-Wrapped Avocado Bites

Dinner: Ultimate Beef Stroganoff

Total for the day:

Calories: 2064; **Carbs:** 26.6 g; **Fibre:** 8.6 g; **Protein:** 103.0 g; **Fat:** 174.3 g

Day 6:

Breakfast: Chicken, Spinach, and Feta Sausage Omelette

Lunch: Cucumber & Smoked Salmon Salad

Snack: Spicy Almond & Cheese Fat Bombs

Dinner: Apple-Glazed Pork Rack

Total for the day:

Calories: 2041; **Carbs:** 25.6 g; **Fibre:** 7.3 g; **Protein:** 104.9 g; **Fat:** 161.9 g

Day 7:

Breakfast: Overnight Chia Pots

Lunch: Ultimate Beef Stroganoff

Snack: Bacon-Wrapped Avocado Bites

Dinner: Apple-Glazed Pork Rack

Total for the day:

Calories: 1887; **Carbs:** 33.5 g; **Fibre:** 15.5 g; **Protein:** 90.8 g; **Fat:** 147.5 g

WEEK 4

Day 1:

Breakfast: Cheesy Bagels

Lunch: Chicken with Roasted Red Pepper Cream

Snack: Buttermilk Biscuits

Dinner: Ginger-Lime Chicken Salad

Total for the day:

Calories: 2144; **Carbs:** 46 g; **Fibre:** 19 g; **Protein:** 120 g; **Fat:** 178 g

Day 2:

Breakfast: Savoury Keto Waffles

Lunch: Ginger-Lime Chicken Salad

Snack: Courgette Fritters (2 serves)

Dinner: Citrus Salmon

Total for the day:

Calories: 1989; **Carbs:** 23.9 g; **Fibre:** 8.8 g; **Protein:** 108.6 g; **Fat:** 153.6 g

Day 3:

Breakfast: Cheesy Bagels

Lunch: Citrus Salmon

Snack: Buttermilk Biscuits

Dinner: Mini Cheeseburger Parcels

Total for the day:

Calories: 1838; **Carbs:** 39 g; **Fibre:** 17.6 g; **Protein:** 101.0 g; **Fat:** 122.3 g

Day 4:

Breakfast: Savoury Keto Waffles

Lunch: Citrus Salmon

Snack: Creamed Spinach (2 serves)

Dinner: Chicken with Roasted Red Pepper Cream

Total for the day:

Calories: 1891; **Carbs:** 21.9 g; **Fibre:** 9.8 g; **Protein:** 89.6 g; **Fat:** 121.0 g

Day 5:

Breakfast: Cheesy Bagels

Lunch: Ginger-Lime Chicken Salad

Snack: Buttermilk Biscuits

Dinner: Mini Cheeseburger Parcels

Total for the day:

Calories: 2144; **Carbs:** 46 g; **Fibre:** 19 g; **Protein:** 120 g; **Fat:** 178 g

Day 6:

Breakfast: Savoury Keto Waffles

Lunch: Mini Cheeseburger Parcels

Snack: Courgette Fritters

Dinner: Ginger-Lime Chicken Salad

Total for the day:

Calories: 1789; **Carbs:** 17.7 g; **Fibre:** 5 g; **Protein:** 96.8 g; **Fat:** 138.1 g

Day 7:

Breakfast: Cheesy Bagels

Lunch: Citrus Salmon

Snack: Buttermilk Biscuits

Dinner: Mini Cheeseburger Parcels

Total for the day:

Calories: 2144; **Carbs:** 46 g; **Fibre:** 19 g; **Protein:** 120 g; **Fat:** 178 g

CHAPTER 3: BREAKFAST AND SMOOTHIES

STRAWBERRY CHANTILLY CRÊPES

Prep time: 15 minutes | Cook time: 25 minutes | Serves 4

- 150g strawberries
- 2 tsp powdered erythritol
- Pinch of sea salt
- 120ml double cream
- ½ tsp vanilla extract
- 1 batch of chocolate crêpes

1. Wash and quarter the strawberries. Sprinkle with 1 teaspoon of erythritol and a pinch of salt. Set aside to macerate.
2. Using a hand whisk or electric mixer, whip the double cream with the remaining teaspoon of erythritol until soft peaks form. Fold in the vanilla extract.
3. Place a tablespoon of the macerated strawberries and a tablespoon of sweetened whipped cream in the centre of each chocolate crêpe. Fold the crêpe in half, then fold again to create a triangle. Serve immediately.

Per Serving

Calories: 378 | Carbs: 10 g | Fibre: 1 g | Protein: 10 g | Fat: 29 g

SPICED SKILLET EGGS WITH YOGURT

Prep time: 15 minutes | Cook time: 20 minutes | Serves 2

- 15ml ghee or extra virgin olive oil
- ½ small yellow onion, thinly sliced
- 1 garlic clove, finely chopped
- 1 tsp smoked paprika
- 1 medium green pepper, sliced
- 120g tinned tomatoes
- 113g fresh spinach (or frozen spinach, well-drained)
- 4 large free-range eggs
- Sea salt and freshly ground black pepper
- 1 tbsp fresh parsley and/or mint, chopped
- Chilli flakes, to taste
- 125g full-fat Greek yoghurt
- 15ml extra virgin olive oil

1. Heat a pan with ghee over medium-high heat. Sauté the onion for 5 minutes until softened. Add garlic, smoked paprika, green pepper, and tomatoes. Cook for a further 5 minutes.
2. Stir in the spinach and cook until just wilted. Season with salt and pepper.
3. Create 4 small wells in the mixture and carefully crack an egg into each. Cover with a lid and cook until the whites are set but the yolks remain runny.
4. Remove from heat and garnish with fresh herbs and chilli flakes. Serve with a dollop of yoghurt drizzled with olive oil.

Per Serving

Calories: 378 | Carbs: 12.7 g | Fibre: 4.2 g | Protein: 21.3 g | Fat: 27.5 g

CHEESY SPINACH AND MUSHROOM SCRAMBLE

Prep time: 10 minutes | **Cook time:** 10 minutes | **Serves** 4

- 50g unsalted butter
- 250g mushrooms, sliced
- 200g fresh spinach
- 8 large free-range eggs
- 100g cheddar cheese, grated
- ½ tsp garlic powder
- Sea salt and freshly ground black pepper, to taste
- Fresh parsley, chopped, for garnish

1. Heat a large frying pan over medium heat and melt the butter. Add the mushrooms and sauté until golden brown, about 6-7 minutes.
2. Add the spinach to the pan and cook until wilted, stirring occasionally.
3. In a bowl, whisk the eggs with garlic powder, salt, and pepper. Pour the egg mixture over the vegetables in the pan.
4. Cook gently, stirring frequently, until the eggs are just set.
5. Sprinkle in the grated cheddar, stirring until melted and fully incorporated.
6. Garnish with fresh parsley and serve immediately.

Per Serving

Calories: 435 | **Carbs:** 6.4 g | **Fibre:** 2.1 g | **Protein:** 25.2 g | **Fat:** 36.8 g

NUT BUTTER CREAM SHAKE

Prep time: 10 minutes | **Cook time:** 5 minutes | **Serves** 2

- 400ml double cream
- 80g powdered erythritol, sifted
- 300ml unsweetened almond milk
- 120g smooth unsweetened almond nut butter, at room temperature
- 2-3 drops liquid stevia (optional)

1. In a large bowl, use an electric whisk to whip the cream and erythritol until soft peaks form.
2. In a separate bowl, use a hand blender to mix the almond milk, nut butter, and liquid stevia (if using).
3. Gently fold the almond milk mixture into the whipped cream until well combined.
4. For best results, cover and refrigerate for at least 2 hours to chill thoroughly.
5. Optional: If you have an ice cream maker, churn the mixture for a more milkshake-like consistency.

Per Serving

Calories: 454 | **Carbs:** 3.7 g | **Fibre:** 0 g | **Protein:** 6.6 g | **Fat:** 46 g

COCONUT AND ALMOND GRANOLA

Prep time: 10 minutes | **Cook time:** 25 minutes | **Serves** 4

- 72g whole almonds
- 54g flaked almonds
- 40g desiccated coconut
- 40g coconut flakes
- 10g chia seeds
- 14g coconut oil
- 3g ground ginger
- 1 tsp vanilla extract
- 12g erythritol
- Pinch of sea salt

1. Preheat the oven to 140°C/Gas Mark 1. Line a baking tray with greaseproof paper.
2. Using a sharp knife, roughly chop the whole almonds, creating a mix of sizes to improve texture. Transfer to a large mixing bowl with the flaked almonds, desiccated coconut, coconut flakes, and chia seeds.
3. Gently melt the coconut oil in a small saucepan or microwave. Pour over the dry ingredients along with the ground ginger, vanilla extract, erythritol, and salt. Mix thoroughly to ensure even coating.
4. Spread the mixture evenly on the prepared baking tray. Bake for 25 minutes, stirring halfway through, until golden and crisp.
5. Remove from the oven and allow to cool completely. Store in an airtight container for up to two weeks.

Per Serving

Calories: 376 | **Carbs:** 16 g | **Fibre:** 8 g | **Protein:** 8 g | **Fat:** 32 g

SAVOURY KETO WAFFLES

Prep time: 5 minutes | **Cook time:** 10 minutes | **Serves** 3

- 4 large free-range eggs
- 110g flavoured cream cheese
- 25g ground almonds
- 1 teaspoon baking powder
- Sea salt and freshly ground black pepper
- Optional toppings: butter, herbs, mozzarella, prosciutto, avocado, bacon

1. In a mixing bowl, whisk together eggs and cream cheese until smooth.
2. In a separate bowl, mix ground almonds and baking powder. Add to the egg mixture and whisk thoroughly to create a lump-free batter.
3. Season generously with salt and black pepper.
4. Preheat and grease the waffle maker according to manufacturer's instructions.
5. Pour in the batter and cook until golden. For best results, wait an extra minute after the indicator suggests the waffles are ready before opening.
6. Serve with your choice of toppings.

Per Serving

Calories: 310 | **Carbs:** 5.5 g | **Fibre:** 0 g | **Protein:** 21 g | **Fat:** 22 g

ITALIAN-STYLE ABUNDANCE BOWLS

Prep time: **15 minutes** | **Cook time:** **15 minutes** | **Serves** **2**

- 15ml ghee or duck fat
- 2 gluten-free Italian sausages (approx. 130g)
- 1 small courgette, spiralised
- 2 large free-range eggs
- 6 cherry tomatoes on the vine (or
- 1 small tomato, halved)
- Sea salt and freshly ground black pepper
- Pinch of chilli flakes
- Fresh basil leaves, to garnish
- Optional: 1 tablespoon homemade pesto

1. Heat a large frying pan over medium heat and add the ghee. Cook the sausages, turning frequently, until browned and cooked through.
2. Create two small nests with the courgette noodles by twirling them around your fingers. Place these beside the sausages in the pan.
3. Crack the eggs into the courgette nests and cook until the whites are just set.
4. In the final moments of cooking, add the tomatoes to the pan and roast for 2-3 minutes (or leave raw if preferred).
5. Season generously with salt, pepper, and chilli flakes. Garnish with fresh basil and add a dollop of pesto if desired.

Per Serving

Calories: **606** | **Carbs:** **7.2 g** | **Fibre:** **2.5 g** | **Protein:** **35.8 g** | **Fat:** **48.2 g**

CREAM-BAKED EGGS

Prep time: **5 minutes** | **Cook time:** **30 minutes** | **Serves** **2**

- 80ml double cream
- 4 large free-range eggs
- Generous pinch of Maldon sea salt flakes
- Pinch of ground white pepper
- Optional: Pinch of your favourite dried herb or spice

1. Preheat the oven to 200°C/180°C fan/Gas Mark 6. Grease two small ramekins.
2. Pour a little cream into each ramekin, then carefully crack two eggs into each.
3. Drizzle the remaining cream over the eggs. Sprinkle with sea salt flakes and white pepper. Add your chosen spice if using.
4. Gently swirl the cream and seasoning with a teaspoon, taking care not to break the egg yolks.
5. Place the ramekins on a baking tray and bake for 25-30 minutes. The eggs will be fully set – this is perfectly normal.
6. Allow to rest for 1 minute before serving. Caution: Ramekins will be extremely hot!

Per Serving

Calories: **351** | **Carbs:** **0.7 g** | **Fibre:** **0 g** | **Protein:** **16 g** | **Fat:** **31 g**

SANDWICH BREAD

Prep time: 10 minutes | **Cook time:** 40 minutes | **Serves** 8

- 195g smooth nut butter (almond or cashew)
- 4 large free-range eggs
- 1 tablespoon low-carb sweetener
- 24g ground almonds or cashew flour
- ¼ teaspoon bicarbonate of soda
- ¼ teaspoon sea salt

1. Preheat the oven to 180°C/Gas Mark 4. Grease a 19x9x7cm loaf tin.
2. In a large mixing bowl, use an electric whisk or stand mixer to blend the nut butter, eggs, and sweetener until smooth and creamy.
3. Sift in the ground almonds, bicarbonate of soda, and salt. Mix until well combined.
4. Pour the batter into the prepared loaf tin, smoothing the top with a spatula.
5. Bake for 40 minutes, or until a skewer inserted into the centre comes out clean.
6. Remove from the oven and allow to cool completely in the tin before turning out.
7. Slice and store in an airtight container in the refrigerator for up to two weeks, or freeze for up to one month.

Per Serving

Calories: 198 | **Carbs:** 5g | **Fat:** 16g | **Protein:** 8g | **Fibre:** 1g

AVOCADO & ALMOND BUTTER POWER SMOOTHIE

Prep time: 5 minutes | **Cook time:** 0 minutes | **Serves** 2

- 1 ripe avocado
- 2 tbsp almond butter (unsweetened)
- 200ml unsweetened coconut milk (or full-fat cream for extra calories)
- 1 tbsp chia seeds
- 2 tbsp coconut oil
- ½ tsp cinnamon
- 1-2 tbsp keto-friendly sweetener (e.g. stevia, monk fruit)
- 4-5 ice cubes (optional)

1. Cut the avocado in half, remove the pit, and scoop the flesh into a blender.
2. Add the almond butter, coconut milk (or cream), chia seeds, coconut oil, cinnamon, and sweetener to the blender.
3. Blend until smooth and creamy.
4. If you prefer a colder smoothie, add ice cubes and blend again.
5. Pour into glasses and serve immediately

Per Serving

Calories: 520 | **Fat:** 46.5 g | **Protein:** 8.2 g | **Carbs:** 7.3 g | **Fibre:** 6.4 g

OVERNIGHT CHIA POTS

Prep time: 5 minutes | Refrigeration time: 8 hours | Serves 2

- 40g whole chia seeds
- 200ml unsweetened almond milk
- 50g fresh blueberries
- 2 tablespoons powdered erythritol
- 2 tablespoons double cream
- 2-3 drops liquid stevia (optional)

1. In a bowl, combine chia seeds and almond milk. Cover and refrigerate overnight. Stir well after 1-2 hours to prevent clumping.
2. In a small saucepan, cook blueberries with a splash of water over medium heat. Crush the berries with a fork, stirring until a thick purée forms and liquid evaporates. Cool completely and refrigerate overnight.
3. In the morning, stir erythritol, double cream, and liquid stevia (if using) into the chia mixture. Gently fold in the blueberry purée.
4. Divide between two serving glasses or pots.

Per Serving

Calories: 258 | Carbs: 13.5 g | Fibre: 9 g | Protein: 6.8 g | Fat: 20.5 g

CHEESY BAGELS

Prep time: 10 minutes | Cook time: 20 minutes | Makes 8 bagels

- 52g coconut flour
- 2 teaspoons baking powder
- 340g low-moisture mozzarella cheese, grated
- 2 large free-range eggs
- Optional toppings: poppy seeds, sesame seeds, sea salt

1. Preheat the oven to 180°C/Gas Mark 4.
2. Line a baking tray with non-stick baking parchment.
3. In a bowl, whisk together coconut flour and baking powder.
4. Melt the cheese in a microwave-safe bowl (30 seconds on high).
5. Add flour mixture and eggs to the melted cheese. Knead into a smooth dough.
6. Divide the dough into 8 equal portions. Roll each into a log about 20cm long and join the ends to form a bagel shape.
7. If using toppings, press each bagel onto the seeds or sprinkle with melted butter or egg wash.
8. Place bagels on the prepared baking tray, leaving 5cm between each.
9. Bake for 15-20 minutes until lightly golden brown.
10. Cool completely. Store in the refrigerator for up to 3 days or freeze for up to 3 months.

Per Serving (2 bagels)

Calories: 368 | Carbs: 12 g | Fat: 22 g | Protein: 26 g | Fibre: 6 g

STRAWBERRY COCONUT SMOOTHIE

Prep time: **5 minutes** | **Cook time:** **10 minutes** | **Serves** **2**

- 140g fresh strawberries, sliced
- ½ tsp vanilla extract
- 425ml full-fat coconut milk
- 1 tbsp fresh lime juice

1. Add all ingredients to a blender.
2. Blend until smooth, adjusting to your preferred consistency.
3. Taste and add extra lime juice if desired.

Per Serving

Calories: **416** | **Carbs:** **10 g** | **Fibre:** **0 g** | **Protein:** **4 g** | **Fat:** **42 g**

CHICKEN, SPINACH, AND FETA SAUSAGE OMELETTE

Prep time: **5 minutes** | **Cook time:** **15 minutes** | **Serves** **1**

- 1 chicken-spinach-feta sausage
- 2 tablespoons olive oil
- 28g mozzarella cheese, grated
- 1 tablespoon finely chopped onion
- 2 tablespoons pine nuts
- 2 large free-range eggs

1. Slice the sausage into rounds. Heat 1 tablespoon of olive oil in a non-stick frying pan and brown the sausage pieces. Remove and set aside.
2. Toast the pine nuts in the same pan for 3-4 minutes until lightly golden. Set aside with the sausage.
3. Whisk the eggs in a bowl.
4. Add remaining olive oil to the pan and cook the omelette. Pour in the eggs.
5. Sprinkle mozzarella over one half, distribute sausage and pine nuts evenly.
6. Cook until cheese melts.
7. Fold and serve.

Per Serving

Calories: **701** | **Fat:** **59 g** | **Protein:** **3 8 g** | **Carbs:** **7 g** | **Fibre:** **2 g**

CHAPTER 4: MAIN DISHES

MINI CHEESEBURGER PARCELS

Prep time: **10 minutes** | **Cook time:** **20 minutes** | **Serves 5**

- 450 g premium beef mince
- 15 g Dijon mustard
- 30 g tomato purée
- 7 g onion powder
- ½ tsp Maldon sea salt
- ¼ tsp freshly ground black pepper
- 10 slices Parma ham
- 60 g small gherkins, quartered
- 70 g mature Cheddar cheese, cut into 10 pieces

1. Preheat oven to 200°C (fan 180°C).
2. Line a baking tray with parchment paper.
3. Mix beef, mustard, tomato purée, onion powder, salt, and pepper in a bowl.
4. Lay Parma ham slice flat. Place 50 g meat mixture on each slice.
5. Press a piece of gherkin and Cheddar into the meat.
6. Wrap Parma ham around filling, placing cheese-side up on baking tray.
7. Bake for 10 minutes until cooked through.

Per Serving

Calories: 461 | **Carbs: 2 g** | **Fibre: 0.6 g** | **Protein: 26.8 g** | **Fat: 26.3 g**

APPLE-GLAZED PORK RACK

Prep time: **5 minutes** | **Cook time:** **30 minutes** | **Serves 4**

- 2 pork racks (about 450g total)
- Maldon sea salt and freshly ground black pepper
- 28g bacon fat or neutral cooking oil
- 240ml chicken stock
- 120ml cider vinegar
- 20g keto-friendly sweetener
- 2 tsp smoked paprika
- 1 tsp Dijon mustard
- ½ tsp minced garlic

1. Season the pork racks generously with Maldon sea salt and black pepper on all sides.
2. Heat a large, heavy-based skillet over medium heat. Add the bacon fat or oil.
3. Brown the pork racks for approximately 5 minutes per side, ensuring a golden colour develops evenly.
4. Transfer the browned pork to a plate. In the same skillet, pour in the chicken stock, cider vinegar, keto sweetener, smoked paprika, Dijon mustard, and minced garlic.
5. Stir thoroughly, scraping up any caramelised bits from the bottom of the pan.
6. Return the pork to the skillet, coating it in the sauce. Reduce heat to low and partially cover the skillet, leaving a small gap for steam to escape.
7. Cook for 15 minutes, then check the sauce consistency. If it's reducing too quickly, add a tablespoon of stock.
8. Flip the pork, replace the lid, and continue cooking for another 15 minutes or until tender.
9. Serve the pork on warm plates, spooning over all the remaining sauce.

Per Serving

Calories: 525 | **Fat: 43 g** | **Protein: 29 g** | **Carbs:6 g** | **Fibre: 1 g**

SALSA VERDE CHICKEN TRAY BAKE

Prep time: 15 minutes | **Cook time:** 40 minutes | **Serves** 4

- 1 medium cauliflower (600 g)
- 240 ml Salsa Verde
- 900 g bone-in chicken thighs (4 large or 8 small)
- Maldon sea salt
- Freshly ground black pepper
- 15 ml ghee or duck fat
- 30-60 ml water

1. Preheat oven to 200°C (fan 180°C).
2. Break cauliflower into florets. Place in baking dish and drizzle with 120 ml Salsa Verde.
3. Pat chicken thighs dry. Season with Maldon sea salt and black pepper.
4. Heat ghee in a large skillet. Sear chicken thighs skin-side down for 5 minutes until golden and crispy.
5. Turn chicken briefly, then place over cauliflower in baking dish.
6. Deglaze skillet with water, pouring contents over cauliflower.
7. Bake for 20-25 minutes, turning halfway. Chicken is done when internal temperature reaches 75°C.
8. Remove from oven and drizzle with remaining Salsa Verde.
9. Serve immediately. Refrigerate leftovers for up to 4 days.

Per Serving

Calories: 590| **Carbs:** 9.2 g | **Fibre:** 3.6 g | **Protein:** 30.9 g | **Fat:** 56.3 g

ROASTED PORK TENDERLOIN WITH CARAWAY SAUERKRAUT

Prep time: 20 minutes | **Cook time:** 45 minutes | **Serves** 8

- 907 g pork loin
- 1 tsp dried dill
- 1 tsp onion powder
- 1 tsp garlic powder
- 15 g Maldon sea salt
- 560 g jarred sauerkraut
- 4 g caraway seeds

1. Preheat oven to 220°C (fan 200°C).
2. Place pork in a roasting tin. Mix dill, onion powder, garlic powder, and sea salt.
3. Sprinkle seasoning evenly over pork. Roast for 40-45 minutes until internal temperature reaches 75°C.
4. Rest pork for 5 minutes before slicing.
5. Meanwhile, warm sauerkraut with caraway seeds in a saucepan.
6. Slice pork thinly and serve atop warm sauerkraut.

Per Serving

Calories: 215 | **Carbs:** 6 g | **Protein:** 33 g | **Fat:** 6 g | **Fibre:** 2 g

SHEPHERD'S CAULIFLOWER MASH

Prep time: 10 minutes | **Cook time:** 10 minutes | **Serves** 4

- 1 kg cauliflower, trimmed and chopped
- 28 g unsalted butter
- ½ tsp Maldon sea salt
- 15-30 ml full-fat coconut milk or double cream

1. Steam or boil cauliflower until tender (fork should glide through easily).
2. Preheat oven to 200°C (fan 180°C).
3. Drain cauliflower thoroughly and allow to cool slightly.
4. Place in food processor with butter, salt, and 15 ml coconut milk.
5. Blend until smooth and creamy, adding extra liquid if needed.
6. Taste and adjust seasoning with extra salt and black pepper.

Per Serving

Calories: 104 | **Carbs:** 11g | **Fat:** 6g | **Protein:** 4g | **Fibre:** 5g

EGG ROLL IN A BOWL

Prep time: 15 minutes | **Cook time:** 20 minutes | **Serves** 4

- 2 tablespoons (30 ml) ghee, duck fat, olive oil, or rapeseed oil
- 4 spring onions, sliced
- 2 garlic cloves, finely chopped
- 500 g minced pork (20% fat)
- 60 ml coconut aminos or tamari sauce
- 500 g ready-prepared coleslaw mix
- 2 tablespoons fresh lime or lemon juice
- Salt and black pepper, to taste
- Optional: 1 teaspoon toasted sesame oil, 2 teaspoons sesame seeds, and lime wedges

1. Heat a large frying pan with the ghee over medium-high heat. Add the white parts of the sliced spring onions and garlic. Cook for 1 minute.
2. Add the minced pork and cook for about 5 minutes, until browned all over. Pour in the coconut aminos, add the coleslaw mix and lime juice. Cook for 5 to 8 minutes, stirring frequently, until the vegetables have wilted and the meat is thoroughly cooked. Remove from the heat and season to taste.
3. Stir through the green parts of the spring onions. Serve immediately, garnishing with sesame oil, sesame seeds, and lime wedges if desired. Can be stored in the refrigerator for up to 4 days.

Per Serving

Calories: 439 | **Carbs:** 10.3 g | **Fibre:** 3.4 g | **Protein:** 23 g | **Fat:** 34 g

'DIRTY RICE' WITH BACON & MUSHROOMS

Prep time: 5 minutes | Cook time: 20 minutes | Serves 4

- 300 g cauliflower florets
- 4 large free-range eggs
- 50 g unsalted butter
- 250 g smoked streaky bacon, finely chopped
- 3 garlic cloves, finely chopped
- 300 g chestnut or mixed mushrooms, sliced
- 6 spring onions, thinly sliced
- Juice of ½ unwaxed lemon
- 10 ml tamari sauce
- Freshly ground black pepper

1. Pulse cauliflower in a food processor until it resembles rice grains. Microwave in a large bowl for 6 minutes. Set aside.
2. Prepare eggs to your preference (soft-boiled or poached recommended).
3. Melt butter in a large non-stick pan over medium heat. Add bacon and garlic, cooking for 9-10 minutes until bacon is crisp and garlic softened.
4. Increase heat to high. Add mushrooms and half the spring onions. Cook for 7-8 minutes until mushrooms caramelise, stirring regularly.
5. Add lemon juice and cauliflower 'rice'. Cook for 2-3 minutes.
6. Stir in tamari sauce and season generously with black pepper.
7. Scatter remaining spring onions over the top and serve with eggs.

Per Serving

Calories: 400 | Carbs: 10.4 g | Fibre: 3 g | Protein: 28 g | Fat: 28 g

CITRUS SALMON

Prep time: 5 minutes | Cook time: 25 minutes | Serves 4

- 2 tsp (10 ml) olive oil
- 454 g salmon, divided into 4 portions
- ½ tsp Maldon sea salt
- ½ tsp freshly ground black pepper
- ½ tsp garlic powder
- 28 g unsalted butter
- 1 tsp powdered erythritol
- 1 tsp orange zest

1. Preheat the oven to 190°C (fan 170°C). Drizzle the olive oil across a non-stick baking tray and arrange the salmon fillets, ensuring they're evenly spaced.
2. Sprinkle Maldon sea salt, black pepper, and garlic powder evenly over the salmon fillets.
3. Melt the butter in a small saucepan over low heat or in the microwave for 20-30 seconds. Stir in the powdered erythritol and orange zest until well combined.
4. Using a pastry brush, generously coat the top and sides of each salmon fillet with the orange-butter mixture.
5. Bake for 20-25 minutes, or until the salmon easily flakes with a fork.
6. Before serving, spoon any remaining butter over the fillets.

Per Serving

Calories: 371 | Carbs: 2 g | Fibre: 1 g | Protein: 25 g | Fat: 16 g

CHICKEN-FRIED STEAK CUTLETS

Prep time: 15 minutes | **Cook time: 60 minutes** | **Serves 4**

- 454 g top round steak, sliced 6 mm thin
- Maldon sea salt
- Freshly ground black pepper
- 50 g pork scratchings (pork rinds)
- 28 g ground almonds
- 1 tsp smoked paprika
- 1 tsp garlic powder
- ½ tsp onion powder
- 1 large free-range egg

1. Preheat oven to 190°C (fan 170°C).
2. Arrange steak slices on a clean surface. Season with Maldon sea salt and black pepper.
3. Blitz pork scratchings, ground almonds, paprika, garlic and onion powders in a food processor until fine.
4. Line a baking tray with parchment paper.
5. Whisk egg in a shallow dish. Transfer crumb mixture to a separate plate.
6. Dip each steak slice in egg, allowing excess to drip off. Press into crumb mixture.
7. Arrange breaded cutlets on prepared tray.
8. Bake for 60 minutes, turning halfway through, until golden and crispy.

Per Serving

Calories: 350 | **Carbs: 3 g** | **Fibre: 1 g** | **Protein: 34 g** | **Fat: 19 g**

ULTIMATE BEEF STROGANOFF

Prep time: 15 minutes | **Cook time: 25 minutes** | **Serves 4**

- 2 rump steaks (140 g each)
- 30 g unsalted butter
- ½ medium onion, finely chopped
- 2 garlic cloves, crushed
- 140 g chestnut mushrooms, thickly sliced
- 60 ml dry white wine
- 150 ml best-quality beef stock
- 150 ml double cream
- 1 tsp Dijon mustard
- Maldon sea salt flakes
- Freshly ground black pepper
- Small bunch fresh flat-leaf parsley, finely chopped

1. Season steaks generously with Maldon sea salt. Slice into thin strips.
2. Melt half the butter in a large, deep non-stick pan over high heat. Sear steak strips until browned and caramelised.
3. Remove beef with a slotted spoon, keeping pan juices. Reduce heat and add onion and garlic, cooking until softened.
4. Add mushrooms and remaining butter. Cook until mushrooms brown and caramelise.
5. Deglaze pan with wine, scraping up any stuck bits. Allow wine to reduce.
6. Pour in beef stock and reduce by two-thirds. Add cream and mustard, cooking until sauce thickens.
7. Return steak strips to pan, warming through for 1-2 minutes.
8. Season with Maldon sea salt and black pepper. Scatter with chopped parsley.

Per Serving

Calories: 694 | **Carbs: 7.8 g** | **Protein: 36 g** | **Fat: 57 g** | **Fibre: 1.2 g**

SPICY LAMB TRAYBAKE WITH CELERIAC ROASTIES

Prep time: 10 minutes | **Cook time:** 35 minutes | **Serves** 4

- 900 g lamb cutlets or chops
- 1 tsp ground cumin
- 1 tsp ground coriander
- Maldon sea salt
- and freshly ground black pepper
- Small bunch fresh flat-leaf parsley, finely chopped

For the Celeriac Roasties:

- 500 g celeriac, peeled and cut into 4 cm chunks
- 25 g unsalted butter
- 1 tsp ground cumin
- 1 tsp ground coriander
- 1 tsp cayenne pepper
- Maldon sea salt

1. Preheat the oven to 200°C (fan 180°C).
2. For the celeriac roasties, bring a large saucepan of salted water to the boil. Add celeriac chunks and cook for 10-12 minutes until partially tender.
3. Drain in a colander and spread on a tray lined with kitchen paper. Allow to steam dry completely.
4. Melt butter in a small saucepan over medium heat. Whisk in cumin, coriander, and cayenne pepper.
5. Pour the spiced butter over the celeriac in a large bowl, tossing gently to coat evenly.
6. Spread celeriac on a large baking tray and roast for 10-12 minutes.
7. Season lamb cutlets with cumin, coriander, and Maldon sea salt.
8. Remove celeriac tray from oven, nestle lamb cutlets amongst the vegetables.
9. Bake for 20-25 minutes until lamb is cooked to your liking and celeriac is golden and tender.
10. Serve immediately, finishing with extra Maldon sea salt, black pepper, and scattered fresh parsley.

Per Serving

Calories: 599 | **Carbs:** 4.9 g | **Fibre:** 1 g | **Protein:** 26 g | **Fat:** 51 g

CHICKEN WITH ROASTED RED PEPPER CREAM

Prep time: 5 minutes | **Cook time:** 10 minutes | **Serves** 2

- 200 g jarred roasted red peppers, drained
- 200 ml double cream
- 10 g unsalted butter
- 3 garlic cloves, finely chopped
- 1 tbsp ras el hanout spice blend
- 400 g leftover roast chicken, roughly chopped
- Small bunch fresh mint leaves
- Maldon sea salt and freshly ground black pepper

1. Blitz roasted red peppers and cream in a food processor until smooth.
2. Melt butter in a non-stick frying pan over medium heat. Sauté garlic for 1-2 minutes until softened.
3. Add ras el hanout and cook briefly until the pan looks dry.
4. Pour in red pepper cream and simmer for 2-3 minutes until slightly reduced.
5. Stir in chicken pieces and warm through. Season with Maldon sea salt and black pepper.
6. Serve scattered with fresh mint leaves.

Per Serving

Calories: 410 | **Carbs:** 8 g | **Fibre:** 2 g | **Protein:** 30 g | **Fat:** 28 g

CREAMY COD WITH JAMMY ONIONS & DILL

Prep time: 5 minutes | Cook time: 30 minutes | Serves 4

- 15 g unsalted butter
- 2 medium onions, very thinly sliced
- 10 ml white wine vinegar
- 300 ml double cream
- 4 skinless cod fillets (140 g each)
- Maldon sea salt and white pepper
- Fresh dill, finely chopped

1. Melt butter in a small pan. Add onions and cook over low heat, stirring occasionally, for 20 minutes until softened and caramelising.
2. Add white wine vinegar and continue cooking for 5-10 minutes until onions become dark and jammy (25-30 minutes total).
3. Preheat oven to 200°C (fan 180°C).
4. Grease a baking dish that fits cod fillets snugly. Spread jammy onions in the base.
5. Warm cream in the same pan used for onions. Season with salt and white pepper.
6. Season cod fillets with salt and white pepper. Place on jammy onions.
7. Pour over warm, seasoned cream.
8. Bake for 20-22 minutes.
9. Serve with Maldon sea salt flakes and a generous scattering of fresh dill.

Per Serving

Calories: 512 | Carbs: 4.8 g| Fibre: 2 g | Protein: 26 g | Fat: 43 g

GARLIC-PARMESAN CHICKEN

Prep time: 10 minutes | Cook time: 15 minutes | Serves 2

- 170 g boneless, skinless chicken thighs
- Maldon sea salt and freshly ground black pepper
- 35 g sliced mushrooms
- 28 ml olive oil
- 30 g fresh spinach leaves
- 60 ml chicken stock
- 60 ml double cream
- ¼ tsp minced garlic
- 15 ml dry white wine (optional)
- 1 packet (225 g) shirataki noodles
- 10 g freshly grated Parmesan cheese, plus extra for serving

1. Cut chicken into 2.4 cm cubes. Season generously with Maldon sea salt and black pepper.
2. Heat a medium-sized non-stick skillet over medium heat. Add olive oil and chicken. Sauté for 3-4 minutes, stirring frequently.
3. Add sliced mushrooms and continue cooking for 2-3 minutes, breaking into bite-sized pieces with a spatula.
4. Add spinach and cook until just wilted, approximately 1-2 minutes.
5. Pour in chicken stock, double cream, and minced garlic. Stir thoroughly. Reduce heat to lowest setting, cover, and simmer.
6. Prepare shirataki noodles according to packet instructions, ensuring thorough draining.
7. Stir Parmesan cheese into the chicken sauce.
8. Serve chicken and sauce over shirataki noodles, garnishing with additional Parmesan if desired.

Per Serving

Calories: 706 | Fat: 61 g | Protein: 32 g | Carbs:5 g | Fibre: 1 g

CHAPTER 5: SALADS AND SOUPS

CURRIED CREAM OF CHICKEN SOUP

Prep time: 5 minutes | **Cook time:** 10 minutes | **Serves** 2

- 14 g butter, divided
- 7 g flaked almonds
- 1½ teaspoons curry powder
- 235 ml chicken stock
- 120 ml tinned coconut milk
- ½ teaspoon chicken stock concentrate (optional)
- Salt and freshly ground black pepper

1. In a medium saucepan over low-medium heat, melt half the butter. Add the almonds and toast until golden brown. Transfer to a small plate and set aside.
2. In the same pan, melt the remaining butter and add the curry powder. Sauté for 1-2 minutes until fragrant. Pour in the chicken stock and coconut milk. Increase heat to medium-high, bring to the boil, then reduce to a gentle simmer.
3. Stir in the stock concentrate (if using) and season with salt and pepper to taste. Serve topped with the toasted almonds.

Per Serving

Calories: 428 | **Fat:** 42 g | **Protein:** 10 g | **Carbs:**8 g | **Fibre:** 2 g

GINGER-LIME CHICKEN SALAD

Prep time: 10 minutes | **Cook time:** 10 minutes | **Serves** 4

- 10 ml olive oil or MCT oil
- 9 g pumpkin seeds (pepitas)
- 30 g MCT Mayonnaise
- 3 g red onion, finely diced
- ½ teaspoon fresh root ginger, grated
- ½ teaspoon garlic, minced
- ½ teaspoon soy sauce
- 1 teaspoon lime juice
- 1 dash sriracha (optional)
- 105 g cooked chicken, diced
- 30 g celery, diced
- Sea salt and freshly ground black pepper

1. Heat a small frying pan over low-medium heat. Add the oil and pumpkin seeds, stirring until golden and slightly puffed, about 4-5 minutes. Remove from heat, sprinkle lightly with sea salt, and set aside.
2. For the dressing, combine the mayonnaise, onion, ginger, garlic, soy sauce, lime juice, and sriracha in a food processor or blender. Blitz until the onion is finely chopped and ingredients are well combined.
3. In a mixing bowl, combine the chicken and celery. Pour over the dressing and mix thoroughly to coat.
4. Transfer to serving plates and top with the toasted pumpkin seeds.

Per Serving

Calories: 728 | **Fat:** 64 g | **Protein:** 37 g | **Carbs:**4 g | **Fibre:** 1 g

AVOCADO & TUNA SALAD

Prep time: 5 minutes | Cook time: 15 minutes | Serves 4

- 3 ripe avocados
- 1 x 160g tin of tuna in olive oil
- 80 ml extra virgin olive oil
- 2 tablespoons fresh lime juice
- 1 cucumber, quartered and sliced
- 1 red onion, thinly sliced
- 2 red peppers, deseeded and sliced
- Sea salt and freshly ground black pepper

1. Drain the tuna, reserving a little of the oil. Using a fork, flake the tuna into generous pieces.
2. In a large serving bowl, combine the avocado, cucumber, onion, and peppers. Gently mix to combine.
3. Add the flaked tuna and fold through the salad ingredients.
4. In a small bowl, whisk together the lime juice and olive oil to create a dressing.
5. Drizzle the dressing over the salad, season with sea salt and black pepper to taste, and serve immediately.

Per Serving

Calories: 639 | Carbs: 7 g | Protein: 44 g | Fat: 45 g | Fibre: 7 g

CUCUMBER & SMOKED SALMON SALAD

Prep time: 10 minutes | Cook time: 10 minutes | Serves 2

- 1 large cucumber (300 g), thinly sliced
- 100 g smoked salmon, sliced
- ½ red onion (50 g), very thinly sliced
- 30 ml extra virgin olive oil
- 15 ml fresh lemon juice
- 5 g fresh dill, finely chopped
- Sea salt and freshly ground black pepper
- Optional: 30 g capers

1. In a large serving bowl, combine the cucumber slices, smoked salmon, and red onion.
2. In a small bowl, whisk together the olive oil, lemon juice, and chopped dill to create a dressing.
3. Pour the dressing over the salad and gently toss to combine.
4. Season with sea salt and black pepper to taste. If using, scatter over the capers.
5. Serve immediately to maintain the salad's freshness and crispness.

Per Serving

Calories: 395 | Carbs: 5.3 g | Fibre: 1.2 g | Protein: 23.4 g | Fat: 21.7 g

LUNCHTIME CHICKEN SOUP

Prep time: 10 minutes | **Cook time:** 15 minutes | **Serves** 8

- 1 × 1.5 kg rotisserie chicken
- 110 g unsalted butter
- 5 carrots, sliced
- 2 onions, finely chopped
- 170 g mushrooms, sliced
- 2 celery stalks, finely chopped
- 140 g green cabbage, shredded
- 2 garlic cloves, minced
- 2 litres chicken stock
- 2 teaspoons dried parsley
- Sea salt and freshly ground black pepper

1. Melt the butter in a large saucepan over medium heat.
2. Add the mushrooms, celery, garlic, and onions. Cook, stirring occasionally, for 4 minutes until softened.
3. Stir in the carrots, dried parsley, chicken stock, and season with salt and pepper.
4. Simmer until the vegetables are tender, approximately 5-7 minutes.
5. Meanwhile, use two forks to shred the rotisserie chicken into bite-sized pieces.
6. Add the shredded cabbage to the soup and stir through.
7. Add the shredded chicken and cook for a further 5-6 minutes to heat through.
8. Taste and adjust seasoning if needed before serving.

Per Serving

Calories: 508 | **Carbs:** 4g | **Protein:** 33g | **Fat:** 40g | **Fibre:** 2g

ROASTED BUTTERNUT SQUASH SOUP

Prep time: 10 minutes | **Cook time:** 10 minutes | **Serves** 4

- 28 g unsalted butter, ghee, or coconut oil
- 1 medium white onion, peeled and diced
- 600 ml chicken stock, vegetable stock, or water
- 4 large garlic cloves, peeled and finely chopped
- 720 g roasted butternut squash, warmed

1. Heat a large frying pan over medium heat and add the butter. Add the onions and cook, stirring occasionally, until they begin to brown and caramelise.
2. Meanwhile, bring the stock to a gentle simmer in a saucepan over low heat. Add the garlic and cook for a few minutes until fragrant.
3. Transfer the butternut squash, onions, garlic, and stock to a liquidiser and blend until smooth.
4. Serve hot. Can be stored in a sealed container in the refrigerator for 2-3 days or frozen for up to 3 months.

Per Serving

Calories: 232 | **Carbs:**28g | **Fat:** 10g | **Protein:** 5g | **Fibre:** 4g

AVOCADO & HALLOUMI SALAD

Prep time: 10 minutes | **Cook time:** 5 minutes | **Serves** 2

- 2 large ripe avocados
- 1 red pepper, finely diced
- ½ red onion, very thinly sliced
- Juice of ½ lemon
- 160 g cherry tomatoes, halved
- 2 tablespoons extra virgin olive oil
- 70 g baby spinach leaves
- 1 portion Brown-buttered Halloumi Fingers
- Sea salt and freshly ground black pepper

1. In a bowl, combine the avocado chunks, red pepper, and red onion. Squeeze over the lemon juice, catching any pips. Toss gently to combine and season with black pepper. Cover and chill in the refrigerator.
2. In a separate bowl, mix the cherry tomatoes with olive oil and a pinch of sea salt flakes. Leave at room temperature.
3. When ready to serve, arrange the baby spinach on a serving plate. Top with the avocado mixture and tomatoes, then finish with the warm halloumi fingers.

Per Serving

Calories: 392 | **Carbs:** 15g | **Protein:** 13g | **Fat:** 34g | **Fibre:** 10g

SUPERFOOD KETO SALAD

Prep time: 20 minutes | **Cook time:** 5 minutes | **Serves** 4

- 120 g baby spinach
- 144 g broccolini, tough ends removed and cut into bite-sized pieces
- 2 garlic cloves, finely chopped
- 2 tablespoons olive oil
- 2 tablespoons tahini
- 2 tablespoons lime juice (from one whole lime)
- ¼ teaspoon salt, plus a pinch
- 1 medium avocado, diced
- 65 g pumpkin seeds, hulled
- 80 g hemp seeds

1. Place the spinach and broccolini in a large mixing bowl.
2. In a small bowl, combine the garlic, olive oil, tahini, lime juice, and a pinch of salt. Mix well.
3. Add the diced avocado to the vegetables and season lightly with salt. Toss to combine.
4. Sprinkle the pumpkin and hemp seeds over the salad, gently mixing through the vegetables.
5. Pour the tahini dressing over the salad and mix thoroughly to coat all vegetables.
6. Allow the salad to rest for 10 minutes before serving to allow the flavours to develop.

Per Serving

Calories: 434 | **Carbs: 11 g** | **Protein: 15 g** | **Fat: 34 g** | **Fibre: 7 g**

AVOCADO & BACON SALAD

Prep time: 10 minutes | **Cook time:** 10 minutes | **Serves** 4

- 8 rashers bacon (160 g), roughly chopped
- 2 medium avocados (240 g), diced
- 100 g mixed salad leaves (rocket, spinach, and watercress)
- 60 g cherry tomatoes, halved
- 30 ml extra virgin olive oil
- 15 ml balsamic vinegar
- Sea salt and freshly ground black pepper
- Optional: 30 g feta cheese, crumbled

1. In a large frying pan, cook the bacon over medium heat for 5-7 minutes until crisp. Transfer to kitchen paper to drain excess fat.
2. In a large mixing bowl, combine the salad leaves, cherry tomatoes, and diced avocado.
3. Add the crispy bacon and gently toss the ingredients together.
4. Drizzle with olive oil and balsamic vinegar, then season with salt and pepper to taste.
5. If using, scatter over the crumbled feta cheese. Serve immediately.

Per Serving

Calories: 380 | **Carbs: 7.5 g** | **Fibre: 5.1 g** | **Protein: 21.6 g** | **Fat: 32.7 g**

BROCCOLI & BLUE CHEESE SOUP

Prep time: 10 minutes | **Cook time:** 20 minutes | **Serves** 2

- 1 litre best-quality chicken stock
- 450 g broccoli florets
- 50 g sour cream
- 50 g blue cheese (such as Stilton)
- 2 tablespoons double cream
- 1 teaspoon mixed seeds, to garnish (optional)

1. Pour the chicken stock into a large, wide saucepan and bring to the boil. Add the broccoli florets and simmer, partially covered, for 10-15 minutes until completely tender.
2. Remove the pan from the heat. Using a hand blender, blitz the mixture directly in the pan until smooth and velvety.
3. Stir in the sour cream and crumble in most of the blue cheese, reserving a little for garnish.
4. Return the pan to a gentle heat and warm through, being careful not to boil.
5. Divide the soup between two warm bowls. Swirl a tablespoon of double cream into each bowl and top with the remaining blue cheese and a scattering of mixed seeds, if using.

Per Serving

Calories: 434 | **Carbs:** 9.1g | **Protein:** 26g | **Fat:** 31g | **Fibre:** 3g

PESTO EGG DROP SOUP

Prep time: 10 minutes | **Cook time:** 20 minutes | **Serves** 6

- 2 litres chicken or vegetable stock
- 340 g dark-leaf Italian kale (or greens of choice: curly kale, chard, collards, Savoy cabbage, or spinach)
- 4 large free-range eggs
- 6 tablespoons fresh pesto
- Sea salt and freshly ground black pepper
- Optional add-ins: cooked chicken, sliced mushrooms, grated Parmesan, additional vegetables (broccoli, cauliflower, carrots)

1. Pour the stock into a large saucepan and heat over medium heat until it begins to simmer. If using any add-in vegetables that require longer cooking, add them now and cook until tender. Add the kale and cook for 1-3 minutes until just wilted.
2. In a separate bowl, whisk the eggs with the pesto. Slowly pour the egg mixture into the simmering soup, stirring continuously. Cook until the egg is just set but still soft. Remove from the heat and season with salt and pepper.
3. Serve immediately, or allow to cool and store in a sealed container in the refrigerator for up to 3 days.

Per Serving

Calories: 188 | **Carbs:** 4.2 g | **Fibre:** 2.2 g | **Protein:** 9.2 g | **Fat:** 16.2 g

SHRIMP & CUCUMBER SALAD WITH LEMON DRESSING

Prep time: **10 minutes** | **Cook time:** **5 minutes** | **Serves** **4**

- 300g cooked shrimp, peeled and deveined
- 1 large cucumber, thinly sliced
- 100g mixed salad greens
- ½ red bell pepper, thinly sliced
- ¼ cup fresh dill, chopped
- 2 tbsp olive oil
- 1 tbsp lemon juice
- 1 tsp Dijon mustard
- Sea salt and freshly ground black pepper, to taste

1. In a large bowl, combine the cooked shrimp, cucumber, salad greens, red bell pepper, and fresh dill.
2. In a separate bowl, whisk together the olive oil, lemon juice, Dijon mustard, salt, and pepper.
3. Pour the dressing over the salad and toss gently to combine.
4. Serve immediately, garnished with extra dill if desired.

Per Serving

Calories: 320 | **Fat: 22.1 g** | **Protein: 26.7 g** | **Carbs: 6.3 g** | **Fibre: 2.1 g**

SEAWEED SALAD

Prep time: **20 minutes** | **Cook time:** **5 minutes** | **Serves** **4**

- 7 g dried wakame seaweed
- 1 medium cucumber, peeled and thinly sliced
- ¾ teaspoon sea salt
- 2 tablespoons rice vinegar
- 1 tablespoon low-carb maple-flavoured syrup (or alternative sweetener)
- 2 teaspoons sesame oil
- 1 teaspoon soy sauce
- 2 teaspoons sesame seeds
- ¼ yellow onion, very thinly sliced
- 1 tablespoon finely grated carrot

1. Place the dried wakame in a bowl and cover with cold water. Leave to rehydrate for at least 15 minutes.
2. In a separate bowl, mix the cucumber slices with ½ teaspoon of salt and set aside.
3. Prepare the dressing by whisking together the rice vinegar, maple-flavoured syrup, sesame oil, soy sauce, and remaining ¼ teaspoon of salt.
4. In a small dry frying pan, toast the sesame seeds over medium heat. Stir constantly until they begin to pop and turn golden brown.
5. Drain the wakame thoroughly. In a serving bowl, combine the wakame, cucumber, onion, and carrot. Pour over the dressing and gently toss. Sprinkle with the toasted sesame seeds before serving.

Per Serving

Calories: 70 | **Carbs: 6g** | **Protein: 1g** | **Fat: 3g** | **Fibre: 2g**

CHAPTER 6: SIDES AND SNACKS

TUNA AVOCADO BOATS WITH LIME

Prep time: 10 minutes | Cook time: 5 minutes | Serves 4

- 260g tinned tuna in brine (drained weight)
- 60g mayonnaise
- 1 tablespoon tamari (gluten-free soy sauce)
- 1 red chilli pepper, finely chopped
- Zest and juice of 1 lime
- 4 handfuls of mixed salad leaves
- 1 tablespoon extra virgin olive oil
- 2 ripe avocados, halved
- Freshly ground black pepper
- Optional: Fresh coriander leaves for garnish

1. In a mixing bowl, combine the tinned tuna, mayonnaise, tamari, finely chopped chilli pepper, lime zest, and a splash of lime juice. Season generously with freshly ground black pepper.
2. In a separate bowl, dress the salad leaves with olive oil, tossing gently to coat.
3. Divide the dressed salad leaves between 4 plates. Squeeze a little extra lime juice over the halved avocados to prevent browning, then season with additional black pepper.
4. Generously top each avocado half with the prepared tuna mixture.
5. If preferred, you can alternatively dice the avocados and mix them directly into the tuna mixture, serving over the dressed salad leaves.

Per Serving

Calories: 332 | Carbs: 5g | Protein: 26g | Fat: 23g | Fibre: 6g

PEANUT BUTTER AND JELLY ICE CREAM

Prep time: 4 hours and 20 minutes, including freezing time | Cook time: 5 minutes | Serves 6

- 142g cream cheese, softened
- 85g unsalted peanut butter
- 1 tsp vanilla extract
- 65g powdered erythritol
- 360ml double cream
- 95g strawberries

1. Add the cream cheese, peanut butter, vanilla extract, and erythritol to a food processor. Blend until well combined. If your peanut butter is soft enough, this mixture can also be beaten together by hand.
2. In a separate mixing bowl, whisk the double cream until fluffy and soft peaks form. This can be done using a stand mixer if preferred. Gently fold the whipped cream into the peanut butter mixture.
3. Add the strawberries to a food processor with 1 tsp water and blend until smooth and pureed.
4. Spoon half of the ice cream mixture into a freezer-proof loaf pan or dish. Drop teaspoonfuls of the strawberry puree randomly over the surface of the Ice cream and gently swirl with a spoon. Repeat this process, adding another layer of ice cream and strawberry puree.
5. Cover and transfer to the freezer for at least 4 hours or until set. Allow the ice cream to soften slightly before serving.

Per Serving

Calories: 405 | Fat: 36g | Carbs: 18g | Protein: 7g | Fibre: 1g

CREAMED SPINACH

Prep time: 5 minutes | **Cook time:** 10 minutes | Serves 4

- 2 teaspoons unsalted butter
- 500g baby spinach leaves
- 1 teaspoon garlic powder
- 100ml double cream
- 100g sour cream
- 50g full-fat cream cheese
- Sea salt and ground white pepper, to taste
- Optional: Fresh nutmeg for grating

1. Melt the butter in a large non-stick pan over medium heat. Add half the spinach and stir continuously until the leaves begin to wilt, making space to add the remaining spinach.
2. Continue cooking until all spinach has completely wilted down. Use a spatula to chop and mash the mixture into a rough purée.
3. Add the garlic powder and cook for a few seconds. Pour in the double cream, sour cream, and cream cheese, stirring to combine.
4. Season with sea salt and white pepper. Continue cooking over medium heat until the creams thicken and the spinach mixture becomes rich and creamy.
5. Optionally, finish with a light grating of fresh nutmeg for added depth of flavour.

Per Serving

Calories: 400 | **Fat:** 27.5 g | **Protein:** 6.8 g | **Carbs:** 3.4 g | **Fibre:** 3.2 g

SALSA CHEESE PARTY DIP

Prep time: 10 minutes | **Cook time:** 10 minutes | Serves 4

- 15ml (1 tablespoon) olive oil
- 6 cherry tomatoes, finely diced
- ¼ small red onion, finely diced
- ½ small red chilli pepper, finely chopped
- ½ teaspoon ground cumin
- ½ teaspoon garlic powder
- 120g (½ cup) cream cheese, softened
- ¼ teaspoon sea salt
- ⅛ teaspoon black pepper
- 113g (1 cup) mature cheddar cheese, grated

1. Heat olive oil in a small pan over low-medium heat. Add tomatoes, red onion, chilli pepper, cumin, and garlic powder. Cook gently for 2-3 minutes until softened and aromatic.
2. Stir in the cream cheese until melted and well combined. Season with salt and pepper.
3. Add grated cheddar and stir until hot, melted, and fully incorporated.
4. Serve warm with low-carb vegetable crudités or prosciutto chips.

Per Serving

Calories: 269 | **Carbs:** 4g | **Protein:** 9g | **Fat:** 22g | **Fibre:** 1g

SPICY ALMOND & CHEESE FAT BOMBS

Prep time: 10 minutes | **Cook time:** 5 minutes | **Makes** 12 fat bombs

- 100g unsalted almonds
- 100g cream cheese, softened
- 50g shredded mozzarella cheese
- 2 tbsp coconut oil, melted
- 1 tsp smoked paprika
- ½ tsp cayenne pepper (adjust to taste)
- ½ tsp garlic powder
- Sea salt to taste

1. Place the almonds in a food processor and pulse until roughly chopped.
2. In a bowl, combine the chopped almonds, cream cheese, mozzarella cheese, melted coconut oil, smoked paprika, cayenne pepper, garlic powder, and sea salt.
3. Mix everything together until well combined. The mixture should be thick and sticky.
4. Roll the mixture into 12 small balls or fat bombs, pressing firmly to hold together.
5. Place the fat bombs on a plate or tray lined with parchment paper and refrigerate for at least 30 minutes to firm up.
6. Serve chilled as a satisfying, high-calorie keto snack.

Per Serving (3 fat bombs)

Calories: 420 | Fat: 38.2 g | Protein: 14.5 g | Carbs: 7.3 g | Fibre: 3.1 g

BUTTERMILK BISCUITS

Prep time: 12 minutes | **Cook time:** 25 minutes | **Makes** 8 biscuits

- 3 large eggs
- 2 tablespoons (27g) coconut oil, solid
- 60ml buttermilk
- ¼ teaspoon sea salt
- 1 teaspoon baking powder
- 1 teaspoon bicarbonate of soda
- 215g ground almonds
- 12g powdered erythritol (such as Swerve)

1. Preheat the oven to 190°C (170°C fan). Line a baking tray with greaseproof paper or a silicone baking mat.
2. In a medium mixing bowl, whisk together the eggs, solid coconut oil, buttermilk, and sea salt. The mixture will appear slightly lumpy.
3. In a large bowl, combine the baking powder, bicarbonate of soda, ground almonds, and powdered erythritol.
4. Add the wet ingredients to the dry ingredients, mixing until just combined. The batter should be thick enough to hold its shape when scooped.
5. Using a cookie scoop or two spoons, divide the mixture into 6 equal portions on the prepared baking tray. Shape each biscuit to be round on top, noting they will not rise significantly during baking.
6. Bake for 20-25 minutes, until the tops and edges are golden brown and the biscuits are set. Allow to cool on the baking tray until comfortable to handle.

Per Serving (2 biscuits)

Calories: 638| Carbs: 22g | Protein: 24g | Fat: 58g | Fibre: 10g

BACON-WRAPPED AVOCADO BITES

Prep time: 10 minutes | Cook time: 15 minutes | Serves 4

- 2 ripe avocados, peeled, pitted, and cut into 8 wedges
- 12 slices of bacon (preferably thick-cut)
- 1 tbsp olive oil
- 1 tsp smoked paprika
- Sea salt and freshly ground black pepper
- 2 tbsp freshly chopped parsley (optional, for garnish)

1. Preheat the oven to 200°C (180°C fan). Line a baking tray with parchment paper.
2. Brush each avocado wedge lightly with olive oil, then season with smoked paprika, salt, and pepper.
3. Wrap each avocado wedge with a slice of bacon, securing it with a toothpick if necessary.
4. Place the bacon-wrapped avocado bites on the prepared baking tray, ensuring the bacon is seam-side down.
5. Bake for 12-15 minutes, until the bacon is crispy and the avocado is warmed through.
6. Remove from the oven and garnish with chopped parsley, if desired. Serve immediately while warm.

Per Serving

Calories: 410 | Fat: 37.5 g | Protein: 12.8 g | Carbs: 6.4 g | Fibre: 4.3 g

BROCCOLI & CHEDDAR SAVOURY MUFFINS

Prep time: 10 minutes | Cook time: 25 minutes | Serves 6

- 200g broccoli florets, steamed and finely chopped
- 100g ground almonds
- 50g mature cheddar cheese, grated
- 4 large eggs, beaten
- 30ml olive oil
- Sea salt and freshly ground black pepper
- ½ teaspoon baking powder

1. Preheat the oven to 180°C (160°C fan). Grease a 6-hole muffin tin with a little olive oil.
2. Steam the broccoli florets until tender, then chop finely.
3. In a large mixing bowl, combine the ground almonds, cheddar cheese, eggs, olive oil, baking powder, salt, and pepper.
4. Fold in the chopped broccoli until evenly distributed.
5. Divide the mixture between the muffin tin compartments.
6. Bake for 20-25 minutes, until the tops are golden brown and a skewer inserted comes out clean.

Per Serving

Calories: 205 | Carbs: 4.2 g | Fibre: 1.8 g | Protein: 11.5 g | Fat: 16.2 g

ROAST BEEF & OLIVE SPINACH ROLLS

Prep time: 5 minutes | Cook time: 5 minutes | Serves 2

- 55g deli roast beef, cut into 4 thick slices
- 34g soft spinach and artichoke cheese spread
- 30g olive tapenade
- 15g baby spinach leaves
- Sea salt and freshly ground black pepper

1. Lay a slice of roast beef on a plate. Spread with 1 tablespoon of spinach and artichoke cheese spread.
2. Spread olive tapenade along one short end of the beef slice. Layer baby spinach leaves across the entire slice.
3. Roll up tightly, starting from the end with the olive spread to ensure it's in the centre.
4. Lightly season with sea salt and black pepper. Repeat with remaining ingredients to create three rolls.

Per Serving

Calories: 297 | Fat: 22 g | Protein: 19 g | Carbs:9 g | Fibre: 9g

COURGETTE FRITTERS

Prep time: 10 minutes | Cook time: 10 minutes | Serves 4

- 2 medium courgettes (400g), grated
- 75g ground almonds
- 2 large eggs, beaten
- 50ml olive oil (or more for frying)
- Sea salt and freshly ground black pepper
- 50g Parmesan cheese, grated
- 1 tsp dried oregano
- 2 tbsp coconut flour (optional for extra texture and calories)
- 30g cream cheese (optional for added richness)

1. Grate the courgettes and use a clean tea towel to squeeze out excess moisture thoroughly.
2. In a mixing bowl, combine the grated courgette, ground almonds, beaten eggs, Parmesan cheese, oregano, coconut flour, and cream cheese (if using). Add salt and pepper to taste.
3. Heat olive oil in a large non-stick frying pan over medium heat.
4. Drop 2-3 tablespoons of the mixture into the pan to form larger fritters. Cook for 4-5 minutes on each side until golden and crisp. Add more oil to the pan as needed for a crispier texture.
5. Drain on kitchen paper to remove excess oil. Serve hot as a snack or side dish.

Per Serving

Calories: 290 | Fat: 25.8 g | Protein: 12.8 g | Carbs: 6.2 g | Fibre: 3.4 g

SPINACH & FETA STUFFED MUSHROOMS

Prep time: 10 minutes | Cook time: 15 minutes | Serves 4

- 8 large button mushrooms (200g), stems removed
- 120g fresh spinach, roughly chopped
- 50g feta cheese, crumbled
- 30ml olive oil
- ¼ teaspoon garlic granules
- Sea salt and freshly ground black pepper

1. Preheat the oven to 180°C (160°C fan).
2. Heat olive oil in a frying pan and sauté the chopped spinach for 2-3 minutes until wilted.
3. Remove from heat and mix in the crumbled feta, garlic granules, salt, and pepper.
4. Carefully fill the mushroom caps with the spinach and feta mixture, arranging them on a baking tray.
5. Bake for 12-15 minutes, until the mushrooms are tender and the filling is golden and slightly crisp.

Per Serving

Calories: 95 | Carbs: 3.1 g | Fibre: 1.4 g | Protein: 5.6 g | Fat: 7.9 g

PINK COLESLAW

Prep time: 15 minutes | Cook time: 45 minutes | Serves 4

- 90g (6 tablespoons) mayonnaise
- 15ml (1 tablespoon) apple cider vinegar
- 15ml (1 tablespoon) fresh lemon juice
- Sea salt and freshly ground black pepper
- Optional: 10g (1 tablespoon) powdered erythritol
- 15g (1 medium) spring onion, finely sliced

Coleslaw Mix

- 175g (2½ cups) white or green cabbage, shredded
- 105g (1½ cups) red cabbage, shredded
- 57g (1 small) carrot, grated

1. Prepare the dressing: In a small bowl, whisk together mayonnaise, vinegar, lemon juice, salt, and pepper. If using, stir in the powdered erythritol.
2. Add most of the sliced spring onion to the dressing, reserving some for garnish.
3. In a large bowl, combine the shredded cabbages and grated carrot.
4. Pour the dressing over the vegetables and toss thoroughly to coat.
5. Cover and refrigerate for 30-60 minutes before serving to allow flavours to develop.

Per Serving

Calories: 193 | Carbs: 6.6 g | Fibre: 2.3 g | Protein: 1.3 g | Fat: 18.8 g

CHEDDAR & CHIVE CAULIFLOWER BITES

Prep time: 10 minutes | **Cook time:** 20 minutes | **Serves** 4

- 1 medium cauliflower (500g), broken into florets
- 100g mature cheddar cheese, grated
- 2 tablespoons fresh chives, finely chopped
- 30ml olive oil
- Sea salt and freshly ground black pepper
- ½ teaspoon garlic granules
- Optional: 30g Parmesan cheese, grated

1. Preheat the oven to 200°C (180°C fan).
2. In a large mixing bowl, toss the cauliflower florets with olive oil, garlic granules, salt, and pepper until evenly coated.
3. Spread the cauliflower on a baking tray in a single layer. Roast for 15-20 minutes, until tender and golden brown.
4. Sprinkle the grated cheddar (and Parmesan, if using) over the roasted cauliflower. Return to the oven for 5 minutes until the cheese is melted and bubbling.
5. Garnish with fresh chives before serving.

Per Serving

Calories: 215 | **Carbs:** 7.2 g | **Fibre:** 3.3 g | **Protein:** 13.7 g | **Fat:** 16.5 g

CUCUMBER & CREAM CHEESE CANAPÉS

Prep time: 5 minutes | **Cook time:** 5 minutes | **Serves** 4

- 1 large cucumber (300g), sliced into 1cm rounds
- 120g full-fat cream cheese
- 2 tablespoons fresh dill, finely chopped
- Sea salt and freshly ground black pepper
- 1 tablespoon chives, finely snipped

1. Slice the cucumber into uniform rounds and arrange on a serving platter.
2. Top each cucumber round with a small dollop of cream cheese.
3. Sprinkle with fresh dill and chives. Season lightly with salt and pepper.
4. Serve immediately as a refreshing nibble or light starter.

Per Serving

Calories: 113 | **Carbs:** 3.6 g | **Fibre:** 1.1 g | **Protein:** 3.4 g | **Fat:** 9.2 g

CHAPTER 7: DESSERTS AND DRINKS

CHOCOLATE AVOCADO MOUSSE

Prep time: **10 minutes** | **Cook time:** **10 minutes** | **Serves** **4**

- 2 medium (400g) ripe avocados, peeled and pitted
- 60ml unsweetened almond milk
- 45g unsweetened cocoa powder
- 30ml liquid stevia or erythritol (adjust to taste)
- 1 tsp vanilla extract
- A pinch of salt
- Optional: 30ml whipped cream, for serving

1. In a blender or food processor, combine the avocados, almond milk, cocoa powder, stevia or erythritol, vanilla extract, and salt.
2. Blend until smooth and creamy, scraping down the sides as needed.
3. Taste and adjust the sweetness if necessary.
4. Spoon the mousse into serving glasses and refrigerate for at least 1 hour to chill and firm up.
5. Serve topped with a dollop of whipped cream, if desired.

Per Serving

Calories: **248** | **Carbs:** **7.2 g** | **Fibre:** **5.4 g** | **Protein:** **3.2 g** | **Fat:** **22.4 g**

VERY BERRY TEA

Prep time: **5 minutes** | **Cook time:** **15 minutes** | **Serves** **1**

- 1 hibiscus tea bag
- 240ml boiling water
- 5 blueberries
- 2 raspberries
- 2 blackberries
- 140g ice cubes

1. In a measuring jug, combine the tea bag and boiling water. Allow the tea to steep for 4 to 5 minutes, or to your preferred strength. Remove the tea bag.
2. Add the blueberries, raspberries, and blackberries to the tea. Place the jug in the refrigerator and chill completely for approximately 15 minutes.
3. Fill a tall glass with ice cubes and pour the chilled berry-infused tea over the top. Serve immediately.

Per Serving

Calories: **6** | **Carbs:** **1g** | **Protein:** **1g** | **Fat:** **1g** | **Fibre:** **1g**

VANILLA CUPCAKES

Prep time: 10 minutes | **Cook time:** 10 minutes | **Makes** 8 cupcakes

- 52g coconut flour
- ¼ tsp baking soda
- ¼ tsp salt
- 4 large eggs
- 76g unsalted butter, melted
- 60g low-carb sweetener (1:1 ratio) or equivalent
- 15ml vanilla extract
- 30ml coconut milk or other milk of choice

1. Preheat your oven to 180°C (fan oven 160°C) or gas mark 4, and line a cupcake tray with cupcake liners.
2. In a bowl, combine the coconut flour, baking soda, and salt. Mix well.
3. In a separate bowl, whisk together the eggs, melted butter, sweetener, vanilla extract, and coconut milk. Add this mixture to the dry ingredients and mix well using a handheld or stand mixer. Let the batter sit for a few minutes and then mix again to ensure everything is well combined.
4. Spoon the batter into the cupcake liners, filling them about three-quarters full. Bake for 20 minutes, or until a toothpick inserted into the centre of a cupcake comes out clean.
5. Allow to cool before frosting.
6. Store the cupcakes in an airtight container at room temperature for up to a few days, in the fridge for a few weeks, or freeze for longer storage.

Per Serving

Calories: 150 | **Carbs:**16g | **Fat:** 6g | **Protein:** 4g | **Fibre:** 2g

RICH BERRY COBBLER

Prep time: 5 minutes | Cook time: 15 minutes | Serves 4

- 55g almond flour
- 25g coconut flour
- 1 medium egg
- 280g fresh blackberries (frozen also works)
- 2 tbsp lime juice
- 2 tbsp powdered erythritol
- 85g butter

1. Preheat your oven to 175°C (fan oven 160°C) and grease a medium-sized pie dish.
2. Add the blackberries to the pie dish, spreading them out evenly.
3. Squeeze the lime juice over the berries and give everything a stir.
4. In a medium bowl, combine all the other ingredients (except the butter) and mix until a crumbly consistency forms.
5. Scatter the crumb mixture over the top of the berries, covering as much of the fruit as possible.
6. Slice the butter into thin pieces and scatter over the top of the cobbler.
7. Place in the oven and bake for 15 minutes, until the top is golden brown.

Per Serving

Calories: 303 | Fat: 27g | Carbs: 5g | Protein: 9g | Fibre: 3g

PICAYUNE PECAN PUDDING

Prep time: 5 minutes | Cook time: 25 minutes | Serves 2

- 1 egg
- 30ml double cream
- 1 tsp sherry
- 20 drops liquid English toffee-flavoured stevia
- ⅛ tsp salt
- 30g erythritol blend
- ½ tsp vanilla extract
- 9g butter
- ½ cup pecans

1. Preheat the oven to 150°C (fan oven 130°C). Grease 2 custard cups with cooking spray or butter.
2. In a food processor or blender, combine all ingredients and pulse until the pecans are chopped to a medium consistency.
3. Divide the mixture evenly between the prepared custard cups. Place the cups in a baking dish or pie plate, then add water to the dish until it reaches just below the rim of the cups (about 1 cm).
4. Bake for 25 minutes. After baking, turn off the oven and let the pudding cool in the water bath until cool enough to handle.
5. Chill in the fridge before serving. Store any leftovers in the fridge for up to 1 week.

Per Serving

Calories: 305 | Fat: 30 g | Protein: 5 g | Carbs:6 g | Fibre: 2 g

CHEESE CRISPS TWO WAYS

Prep time: 5 minutes | Cook time: 15 minutes | Serves 4

Parmesan Cheese Crisps

- 90 g grated Parmesan cheese
- 4 g fresh thyme leaves or 1 teaspoon dried thyme
- 4 pieces (14 g) sun-dried tomatoes or black olives, chopped

Cheddar Cheese Crisps

- 113 g grated mature Cheddar cheese
- 1 small fresh jalapeño pepper, thinly sliced (or pickled jalapeños)
- 28g Spanish chorizo or pepperoni, finely sliced

1. Preheat the oven to 210°C (fan) or 230°C (conventional). Line a baking tray with greaseproof paper.
2. Divide the cheese into 8 individual mounds on the prepared baking tray, ensuring approximately 5 cm space between each mound to allow for spreading. Top each cheese mound with the respective ingredients.
3. Transfer to the oven and bake for 7-10 minutes, until the cheese has melted and is beginning to crisp around the edges.

Per Serving

Calories: 148 | Carbs: 1.6 g | Fibre: 0.2 g | Protein: 8.2 g | Fat: 12.2 g

COFFEE ALMOND FLOAT

Prep time: 5 minutes | Cook time: 5 minutes | Serves 1

- 1 cup brewed coffee, chilled (bottled cold brew works well)
- 175ml canned coconut milk
- 2 tsp cocoa powder
- ¼ tsp almond extract
- 18 drops dark chocolate-flavoured liquid stevia
- 355ml diet cream soda, chilled
- 60ml heavy cream, chilled and whipped

1. Combine the chilled coffee, coconut milk, cocoa powder, almond extract, and liquid stevia in a blender. Blend for a few seconds until fully combined.
2. Pour into a glass, then add the chilled cream soda.
3. Top with the whipped cream and serve immediately.

Per Serving

Calories: 276 | Fat: 29 g | Protein: 3 g | Carbs:5 g | Fibre: 1 g

STRAWBERRIES & CREAM LOLLIES

Prep time: 5 minutes | Freeze time: 6 hours | Serves 6

- 250g trimmed strawberries, finely diced
- 250ml double cream
- 3 tbsp powdered erythritol, sifted
- 2–3 drops liquid stevia (optional)

1. Place the diced strawberries in a bowl and lightly mash them using the back of a fork.
2. In a separate bowl, use a hand mixer to whip the double cream and erythritol to semi-stiff peaks.
3. Fold the mashed strawberries and stevia (if using) into the whipped cream mixture.
4. Spoon the mixture into 6 lolly moulds (100ml capacity), tapping the moulds on the worktop to remove any air pockets.
5. Freeze overnight or for at least 6 hours. Remove from the freezer about 30 minutes before serving.

Per Serving

Calories: 214 | Carbs: 3.7g | Protein: 0.9g | Fat: 21g | Fibre: 1g

LITTLE RASPBERRY MOUSSE POTS

Prep time: 10 minutes | Cook time: 5 minutes | Serves 6

- 2 tablespoons boiling water
- 1½ teaspoons gelatine powder
- 280g fresh raspberries, plus extra for garnish
- 1 teaspoon fresh lemon juice
- 230ml double cream
- 3 tablespoons powdered erythritol

1. In a small ramekin, sprinkle the gelatine powder over boiling water. Allow to stand for 3-4 minutes until completely dissolved. Set aside.
2. Place raspberries and lemon juice in a small food processor and blitz until smooth. Transfer the purée to a small saucepan over low heat.
3. Add the dissolved gelatine to the raspberry purée, stirring well and cooking for 30-40 seconds to incorporate.
4. In a large mixing bowl, use an electric hand mixer to whip the double cream and erythritol until soft peaks form.
5. Gently fold the raspberry purée into the whipped cream until well combined.
6. Divide the mixture between 6 small dessert glasses or ramekins.
7. Refrigerate, covered, for at least 2 hours until set. Garnish with additional fresh raspberries before serving, if desired.

Per Serving

Calories: 206 | Carbs: 3.2g | Protein: 2.2g | Fat: 20g | Fibre: 1g

LOW CARB BROWNIES

Prep time: 5 minutes | Cook time: 15 minutes | Serves 12

- 80ml almond butter
- 170g softened butter
- 3 medium eggs
- 30g cocoa powder
- 160g erythritol
- 110g almond flour
- ½ tsp instant coffee powder
- 28g chopped dark chocolate
- ½ tsp baking powder
- ½ tsp salt
- 1 tbsp vanilla extract
- 2 tbsp water

1. Preheat the oven to 175°C (fan oven 160°C) and line a large baking dish with parchment paper.
2. Use a hand mixer to combine the almond butter, eggs, butter, and erythritol until everything is thoroughly mixed.
3. Add the baking powder, cocoa powder, almond flour, vanilla extract, water, salt, and coffee powder. Mix again until well combined.
4. Stir in the chopped chocolate.
5. Transfer the mixture to the prepared baking dish and smooth the top.
6. Bake for 25 minutes, then allow to cool for 30 minutes before cutting into squares.

Per Serving

Calories: 120 | Carbs: 1g | Protein: 3g | Fat: 11g | Fibre: 2g

DOUBLE CREAMY COFFEE

Prep time: 2 minutes | Cook time: 2 minutes | Serves 1

- 40ml double cream
- 1 tablespoon collagen protein powder
- 1 teaspoon MCT oil
- Sweetener of choice (optional)
- 1 serving of freshly brewed black coffee

1. In a coffee mug, combine the double cream, collagen powder, and MCT oil. If you prefer sweetened coffee, add your chosen sweetener.
2. Use a milk frother or small whisk to blend the ingredients thoroughly.
3. Brew your coffee directly into the mug or pour hot coffee over the cream mixture.
4. Whisk once more to ensure everything is well combined and enjoy immediately.

Per Serving

Calories: 259 | Carbs: 0.6g | Protein: 8g | Fat: 25g | Fibre: 0g

HOT CHOCOLATE

Prep time: 5 minutes | Cook time: 10 minutes | Serves 4

- 360ml double cream
- 360ml tepid water
- 100g dark chocolate (85% cocoa), roughly chopped
- 1½ tablespoons unsweetened cocoa powder
- 1 tablespoon powdered erythritol
- 2-3 drops liquid stevia (optional)
- Unsweetened cocoa powder, for dusting (optional)
- Whipped cream, for topping (optional)

1. In a medium saucepan, combine all hot chocolate ingredients over the lowest possible heat. Allow the ingredients to melt and warm through gently.
2. Whisk the mixture carefully to ensure all ingredients are well combined and smooth. Taste and adjust sweetness if required.
3. Divide the hot chocolate between 4 mugs.
4. If desired, top with a dollop of whipped cream and dust lightly with cocoa powder.

Per Serving

Calories: 253 | Carbs: 7g | Protein: 2g | Fat: 23g | Fibre: 3g

ESPRESSO BROWNIES

Prep time: 10 minutes | Cook time: 25 minutes | Serves 16

- 48g ground almonds
- 30g unsweetened cocoa powder
- 60g low-carb granulated sweetener
- ½ teaspoon sea salt
- ½ teaspoon baking powder
- ½ teaspoon espresso powder or 1 tablespoon instant coffee granules
- ½ teaspoon vanilla extract
- 112g unsalted butter, melted
- 3 large free-range eggs

1. Preheat the oven to 180°C (160°C fan)/Gas Mark 4.
2. Lightly grease a 20 × 20cm square baking tin with butter or line with parchment paper.
3. In a large mixing bowl, whisk together the ground almonds, cocoa powder, sweetener, salt, baking powder, and espresso powder until thoroughly combined.
4. In a separate bowl, mix the melted butter, vanilla extract, and eggs until well blended.
5. Pour the wet ingredients into the dry ingredients and whisk until you have a smooth batter.
6. Transfer the batter to the prepared baking tin, using a spatula to spread it evenly.
7. Bake for 15-18 minutes, or until a skewer inserted into the centre comes out mostly clean.
8. Allow to cool completely in the tin before cutting into 16 squares.

Per Serving

Calories: 109 | Carbs:10g | Fat: 7g | Protein: 2g | Fibre: 1g

CHAPTER 8: BASES, CONDIMENTS AND SAUCES

EASY NO-SUGAR-ADDED KETCHUP

Prep time: 5 minutes | Cook time: 15 minutes | Serves 8

- 425g can tomato sauce
- 120ml cider vinegar
- 45g erythritol blend
- 1 tsp salt
- ½ tsp onion powder
- ¼ tsp garlic powder

1. Combine all ingredients in a non-reactive saucepan (such as stainless steel, ceramic nonstick, or enamelware). Bring to a simmer.
2. Let it cook for 15 minutes, then allow to cool. Once cooled, transfer to a squeeze-type ketchup bottle using a funnel, or store in a jar or snap-top container.
3. Keep in the fridge, where it will last indefinitely.

Per Serving

Calories: 6 | Fat: 0 g | Protein: 0 g | Carbs: 2 g | Fibre: 2 g

HOMEMADE MAYONNAISE

Prep time: 5 minutes | Cook time: 5 minutes | Serves 10

- 1 large egg yolk
- 2 tsp white wine vinegar
- 1 tsp Dijon mustard
- 150ml light olive oil (or avocado oil)
- Salt, to taste

1. Place the egg yolk, vinegar, and mustard in a small jug. Use a small whisk to combine thoroughly. (For stability, place the jug on a damp cloth to prevent it from moving while you whisk.)
2. Drizzle small amounts of oil into the mixture at a time, whisking well between each addition until emulsified. It's important to add the oil gradually to avoid the mixture splitting.
3. Once all the oil has been incorporated and the mixture is thick, smooth, and creamy, taste and adjust seasoning with salt.
4. Cover and store in the fridge for no longer than 4 days.

Per Serving

Calories: 276 | Fat: 6 g | Carbs: 0g | Protein: 0.7g | Fat 30g

CHICKEN BROTH

Prep time: 10 minutes | **Cook time:** 2 hours 40 minutes | **Serves** 8

- 1.6kg raw chicken carcasses
- 10g lard
- 2 celery stalks, roughly chopped
- 1 large onion, roughly chopped
- 3 garlic cloves
- ½ tsp whole black peppercorns
- 1 bay leaf
- 2.5 litres cold water
- Salt flakes, to serve

1. Preheat your oven to 220°C/200°C fan/425°F/gas mark 7.
2. Spread the chicken carcasses on a large baking tray and roast for 40 minutes until golden. Remove from the oven and set aside.
3. Melt the lard in a pressure cooker over a high heat. Add the celery and onion and fry until caramelised.
4. Add the roasted chicken carcasses, including all rendered fat and juices from the tray, to the pressure cooker. Smash the garlic cloves with the back of a knife and add to the pot along with the black peppercorns and bay leaf. Add the cold water and bring to the boil, skimming off any impurities that rise to the surface.
5. Reduce the heat to medium and secure the lid of the pressure cooker. Cook for 2 hours.
6. Once cooked, allow the pressure cooker to cool completely before safely decompressing. Strain the broth through a fine mesh sieve into a large bowl, discarding the vegetables and bones.
7. Let the broth cool, then place it in the fridge overnight to allow the fat to solidify on the surface. This makes it easier to remove.
8. Reheat the broth as needed, adding salt to taste for added flavour.

Per Serving

Calories: 415 | **Carbs:** 5.3 g | **Fibre:** 0 g | **Protein:** 15 g | **Fat:** 35 g

PEANUT SAUCE

Prep time: 5 minutes | **Cook time:** 0 minutes | **Serves** 6

- 120ml canned coconut milk
- 65g natural peanut butter (smooth)
- 1 tsp minced garlic
- 1 tbsp soy sauce
- 1 tsp fish sauce
- 1 tsp lemon juice
- ½ tsp dark sesame oil
- ¼ tsp dried red pepper flakes
- 4 drops English toffee-flavoured liquid stevia

1. Combine all ingredients in a food processor and blend until smooth and well combined.
2. Store in an airtight container in the fridge for up to 5 days.

Per Serving

Calories: 106 | **Fat:** 9 g | **Protein:** 3 g | **Carbs:** 3 g | **Fibre:** 1 g

GARLIC BUTTER SAUCE

Prep time: 5 minutes | **Cook time:** 5 minutes | **Serves** 4

- 115g unsalted butter
- 3 cloves garlic, minced
- 1 tbsp fresh lemon juice
- 1 tbsp fresh parsley, chopped
- Salt and pepper, to taste

1. Melt the butter in a small saucepan over medium heat.
2. Add the minced garlic and sauté for 1-2 minutes until fragrant.
3. Stir in the lemon juice, parsley, salt, and pepper.
4. Serve warm over grilled meats, vegetables, or as a dipping sauce.

Per Serving

Calories: 168 | **Carbs:** 0.4 g | **Fibre:** 0 g | **Protein:** 0.4 g | **Fat:** 18.4 g

SUGAR-FREE BBQ SAUCE

Prep time: 10 minutes | **Cook time:** 15 minutes | **Serves** 6

- 240ml sugar-free tomato ketchup
- 30ml apple cider vinegar
- 15ml Worcestershire sauce
- 15g Dijon mustard
- ½ tsp smoked paprika
- Salt and pepper, to taste

1. In a saucepan, combine all the ingredients and bring to a simmer over medium heat.
2. Reduce the heat and let the sauce cook for 10-15 minutes, stirring occasionally, until thickened.
3. Adjust seasoning and serve with grilled meats or as a dipping sauce.

Per Serving (2 tablespoons)

Calories: 35 | **Carbs:** 2.1 g | **Fibre:** 0.5 g | **Protein:** 0.5 g | **Fat:** 1.7 g

TARTAR SAUCE

Prep time: 5 minutes | Cook time: 5 minutes | Serves 6

- 120g mayonnaise
- 30g dill pickle relish
- 1 tsp Dijon mustard
- 1 tsp fresh lemon juice
- Salt and pepper, to taste

1. In a small bowl, mix together the mayonnaise, pickle relish, Dijon mustard, and lemon juice.
2. Season with salt and pepper to taste.
3. Serve with fish, seafood, or as a dip.

Per Serving (2 tablespoons)

Calories: 119 | Carbs: 2.2 g | Fibre: 0.2 g | Protein: 0.5 g | Fat: 11.4 g

KETO PESTO

Prep time: 10 minutes | Cook time: 5 minutes | Serves 4

- 50g fresh basil leaves
- 30g pine nuts
- 60ml olive oil
- 25g grated Parmesan cheese
- 1 garlic clove, minced
- Salt and pepper, to taste

1. In a food processor, combine the basil, pine nuts, garlic, and Parmesan.
2. With the processor running, slowly pour in the olive oil until smooth.
3. Season with salt and pepper to taste.
4. Serve as a dip, or drizzle over vegetables, meats, or salads.

Per Serving (2 tablespoons)

Calories: 202 | Carbs: 2.1 g | Fibre: 0.5 g | Protein: 6.9 g | Fat: 19.6 g

SWEET CHILI SAUCE

Prep time: **5 minutes** | **Cook time:** **15 minutes** | **Serves 6**

- 120ml apple cider vinegar
- 30g erythritol
- 60ml water
- 15ml fish sauce
- ½ tsp xanthan gum
- ½ tsp chili flakes

1. In a saucepan, combine vinegar, erythritol, water, and fish sauce. Bring to a boil.
2. Reduce the heat and whisk in xanthan gum until the sauce thickens.
3. Stir in chili flakes and cook for 1-2 more minutes.
4. Let cool and serve with chicken wings or grilled meats.

Per Serving (2 tablespoons)

Calories: **12** | **Carbs:** **2.3 g** | **Fibre:** **0 g** | **Protein:** **0 g** | **Fat:** **0 g**

RANCH DRESSING

Prep time: **5 minutes** | **Cook time:** **5 minutes** | **Serves 10**

- 240ml sour cream
- 120ml mayonnaise
- 15ml lemon juice
- ½ tsp garlic powder
- ½ tsp onion powder
- 10g fresh chives, chopped
- Salt and pepper, to taste

1. In a bowl, whisk together the sour cream, mayonnaise, lemon juice, garlic powder, onion powder, and chives.
2. Season with salt and pepper to taste.
3. Store in an airtight container in the fridge for up to 1 week.

Per Serving (1 tablespoon)

Calories: **80** | **Carbs:** **1.2 g** | **Fibre:** **0.2 g** | **Protein:** **0.8 g** | **Fat:** **8.2 g**

HOLLANDAISE SAUCE

Prep time: 5 minutes | Cook time: 5 minutes | Serves 4

- 115g unsalted butter
- 3 large egg yolks (approx. 180g)
- 15ml fresh lemon juice
- ¼ tsp Dijon mustard
- Salt and pepper, to taste

1. In a small saucepan, melt the butter over low heat.
2. In a separate bowl, whisk together the egg yolks, lemon juice, mustard, and a pinch of salt.
3. Slowly drizzle the melted butter into the egg mixture, whisking constantly, until smooth and creamy.
4. Serve immediately over asparagus, eggs, or seafood.

Per Serving (2 tablespoons)

Calories: 188 | Carbs: 0.3 g | Fibre: 0 g | Protein: 2.6 g | Fat: 18.5 g

AVOCADO SALSA

Prep time: 10 minutes | Cook time: 5 minutes | Serves 4

- 2 ripe avocados (approx. 300g), diced
- 50g red onion, finely chopped
- 100g tomato, diced
- 15ml fresh lime juice
- 5g fresh coriander, chopped
- 1 small red chilli, finely chopped (optional)
- Salt and pepper, to taste

1. In a bowl, combine the diced avocados, red onion, tomato, lime juice, coriander, and chilli (if using).
2. Gently stir everything together, making sure the avocado stays mostly intact.
3. Season with salt and pepper to taste.
4. Serve immediately as a topping for grilled meats, fish, or as a refreshing dip with low-carb crisps.

Per Serving (2 tablespoons)

Calories: 95 | Carbs: 4.6 g | Fibre: 3.4 g | Protein: 1.3 g | Fat: 8.2 g

KETO MUSTARD

Prep time: 5 minutes | **Cook time:** 5 minutes | **Serves** 8

- 60ml Dijon mustard
- 30ml apple cider vinegar
- 15ml olive oil
- ½ tsp turmeric
- ¼ tsp garlic powder
- Salt and pepper, to taste

1. In a small bowl, combine the Dijon mustard, apple cider vinegar, olive oil, turmeric, and garlic powder.
2. Whisk until smooth and season with salt and pepper.
3. Store in an airtight container in the fridge for up to 1 week.

Per Serving (1 tablespoon)

Calories: 15 | **Carbs:** 0.5 g | **Fibre:** 0 g | **Protein:** 0.3 g | **Fat:** 1.3 g

CAESAR DRESSING

Prep time: 5 minutes | **Cook time:** 5 minutes | **Serves** 8

- 120g mayonnaise
- 60ml olive oil
- 30ml fresh lemon juice
- 15g Dijon mustard
- 1 clove garlic, minced
- 20g grated Parmesan cheese
- Salt and pepper, to taste

1. In a bowl, whisk together the mayonnaise, olive oil, lemon juice, mustard, garlic, and Parmesan.
2. Season with salt and pepper to taste.
3. Serve with a classic Caesar salad or as a dip.

Per Serving (2 tablespoons)

Calories: 139 | **Carbs:** 1.5 g | **Fibre:** 0.2 g | **Protein:** 2.4 g | **Fat:** 14.1 g

MEASUREMENT CONVERSION CHART

VOLUME EQUIVALENTS(DRY)

US STANDARD	METRIC (APPROXIMATE)
1/8 teaspoon	0.5 mL
1/4 teaspoon	1 mL
1/2 teaspoon	2 mL
3/4 teaspoon	4 mL
1 teaspoon	5 mL
1 tablespoon	15 mL
1/4 cup	59 mL
1/2 cup	118 mL
3/4 cup	177 mL
1 cup	235 mL
2 cups	475 mL
3 cups	700 mL
4 cups	1 L

VOLUME EQUIVALENTS(LIQUID)

US STANDARD	US STANDARD (OUNCES)	METRIC (APPROXIMATE)
2 tablespoons	1 fl.oz.	30 mL
1/4 cup	2 fl.oz.	60 mL
1/2 cup	4 fl.oz.	120 mL
1 cup	8 fl.oz.	240 mL
1 1/2 cup	12 fl.oz.	355 mL
2 cups or 1 pint	16 fl.oz.	475 mL
4 cups or 1 quart	32 fl.oz.	1 L
1 gallon	128 fl.oz.	4 L

TEMPERATURES EQUIVALENTS

FAHRENHEIT(F)	CELSIUS(C) (APPROXIMATE)
225 °F	107 °C
250 °F	120 °C
275 °F	135 °C
300 °F	150 °C
325 °F	160 °C
350 °F	180 °C
375 °F	190 °C
400 °F	205 °C
425 °F	220 °C
450 °F	235 °C
475 °F	245 °C
500 °F	260 °C

WEIGHT EQUIVALENTS

US STANDARD	METRIC (APPROXIMATE)
1 ounce	28 g
2 ounces	57 g
5 ounces	142 g
10 ounces	284 g
15 ounces	425 g
16 ounces (1 pound)	455 g
1.5 pounds	680 g
2 pounds	907 g

The Dirty Dozen and Clean Fifteen

The Environmental Working Group (EWG) is a nonprofit, nonpartisan organization dedicated to protecting human health and the environment Its mission is to empower people to live healthier lives in a healthier environment. This organization publishes an annual list of the twelve kinds of produce, in sequence, that have the highest amount of pesticide residue-the Dirty Dozen-as well as a list of the fifteen kinds ofproduce that have the least amount of pesticide residue-the Clean Fifteen.

THE DIRTY DOZEN	THE CLEAN FIFTEEN
• The 2016 Dirty Dozen includes the following produce. These are considered among the year's most important produce to buy organic:	• The least critical to buy organically are the Clean Fifteen list. The following are on the 2016 list:

THE DIRTY DOZEN

Strawberries	Spinach
Apples	Tomatoes
Nectarines	Bell peppers
Peaches	Cherry tomatoes
Celery	Cucumbers
Grapes	Kale/collard greens
Cherries	Hot peppers

THE CLEAN FIFTEEN

Avocados	Papayas
Corn	Kiw
Pineapples	Eggplant
Cabbage	Honeydew
Sweet peas	Grapefruit
Onions	Cantaloupe
Asparagus	Cauliflower
Mangos	

• The Dirty Dozen list contains two additional itemskale/collard greens and hot peppers-because they tend to contain trace levels of highly hazardous pesticides.

• Some of the sweet corn sold in the United States are made from genetically engineered (GE) seedstock. Buy organic varieties of these crops to avoid GE produce.

APPENDIX 3: INDEX

Hey there!

Wow, can you believe we've reached the end of this culinary journey together? I'm truly thrilled and filled with joy as I think back on all the recipes we've shared and the flavors we've discovered. This experience, blending a bit of tradition with our own unique twists, has been a journey of love for good food. And knowing you've been out there, giving these dishes a try, has made this adventure incredibly special to me.

Even though we're turning the last page of this book, I hope our conversation about all things delicious doesn't have to end. I cherish your thoughts, your experiments, and yes, even those moments when things didn't go as planned. Every piece of feedback you share is invaluable, helping to enrich this experience for us all.

I'd be so grateful if you could take a moment to share your thoughts with me, be it through a review on Amazon or any other place you feel comfortable expressing yourself online. Whether it's praise, constructive criticism, or even an idea for how we might do things differently in the future, your input is what truly makes this journey meaningful.

This book is a piece of my heart, offered to you with all the love and enthusiasm I have for cooking. But it's your engagement and your words that elevate it to something truly extraordinary.

Thank you from the bottom of my heart for being such an integral part of this culinary adventure. Your openness to trying new things and sharing your experiences has been the greatest gift.

Catch you later,

Judy K. Silas

Printed in Great Britain
by Amazon

56227568R00044